Basic Concepts of
Vector Algebra in 2D and 3D

Basic Concepts of
Vector Algebra in 2D and 3D

Chanchal Dass, FIE

Published by:

Dass Scientific Research Labs Private Limited,
F 201 Parth Avenue, Chandkheda,
Ahmedabad, Gujarat,
India.

Email: cdass01@gmail.com
Mobile: +91-8320172787

Publishing Platform: Notion Press
Book Format: Paperback
Published on: 27th December, 2024
Edition: International Edition

Price: INR 1000/-

Website: www.dassmath.com

Dedication

To my mother, **Nalinibala**, who has taught me to enjoy the real beauty of this universe and enjoy it in all situation.

To my father, **Bhabesh Chandra**, who taught me to stand firm in all odd situations of life.

To my wife, **Bela**, for her unconditional love and sailing with me silently during our turbulent days.

To all my brothers, **Shyamal**, **Kamal**, **Parimal**, **Utpal**, and my sister **Manju**, for their support towards me during my formative days.

To all my family members and friends for their love, affection, and support all the time throughout my life.

Chanchal Dass, FIE

What am I trying to do?

At present, for one, mathematics means numbers, symbols, equations, and formulas. I am trying to change this perception to points, line, surfaces, and solids.

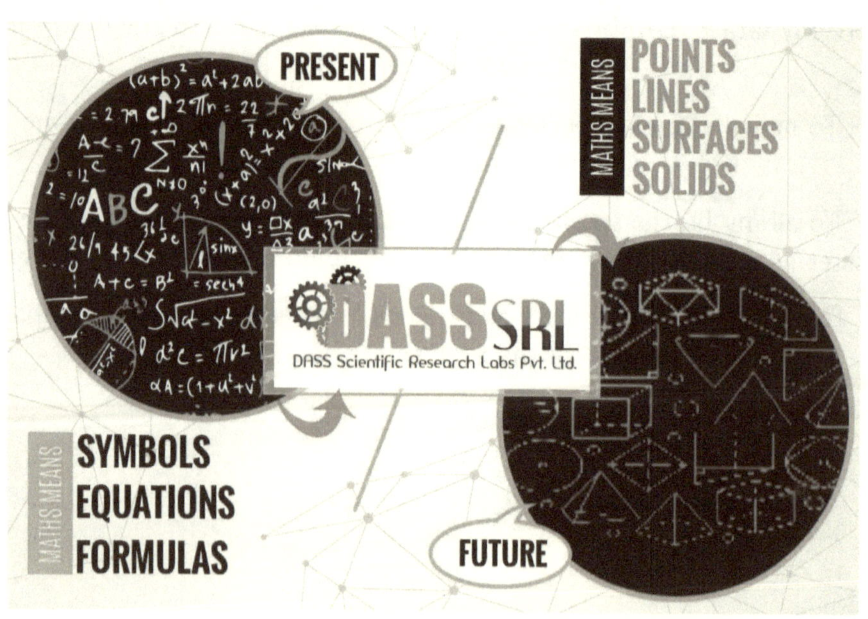

Contents

CONTENTS ix

List of Tables

List of Figures

Preface

In the journey of learning mathematics, especially as students advance to higher levels, understanding abstract concepts becomes crucial. Too often, mathematics is presented as a series of problems to be solved, with the underlying concepts being treated as secondary. This approach can leave students feeling disconnected from the true essence of the subject. My goal in writing this book, Vector Algebra, is to shift the focus back to where it belongs—on the concepts themselves.

This book is designed to guide students through the foundational principles of vector algebra, one concept at a time. By breaking down each topic into its essential components, I aim to provide a clear and thorough understanding of the subject, free from the distractions of premature problem-solving. Instead of diving into complex problems, this book encourages students to first grasp the concepts deeply, ensuring that they can apply their knowledge with confidence when the time comes.

The structure of this book reflects this philosophy. Starting with the basic definitions and properties of vectors, I progressively introduce more advanced operations and applications, such as vector addition, scalar multiplication, and the use of vectors in three-dimensional geometry. Each chapter builds on the last, allowing students to develop their understanding in a logical and coherent manner.

Another unique feature of this book is its emphasis on visualization. To help students internalize the concepts, I have included sections on geometric modeling and animation using MS Excel. This approach not only enhances comprehension but also makes learning more interactive and engaging, allowing students to see the real-world implications of the abstract ideas they are studying.

My hope is that this book will serve as a valuable resource for students who seek to master vector algebra by truly understanding the concepts, rather than just memorizing procedures. Whether you are a student preparing for exams or a teacher looking for a more concept-driven approach to teaching vector algebra, this book is for you.

I would like to express my deep appreciation to everyone who has supported me in bringing this book to life. Your encouragement has been invaluable. It is my sincere wish that this book will help students unlock the beauty and power of vector algebra through a deeper conceptual understanding.

Chanchal Dass, FIE,
15th August, 2024.

Acknowledgements

I hereby convey my sincere gratitude to the persons who have provided guidance and support to develop the new system of teaching mathematics and help me promoting this technique globally:

1. Dr. Ranadhir Mukhopadhaya, Former Chief Scientist, National Institute of Oceanography, Goa,

2. Dr. Asim Banerjee, Dhirubhai Ambani Institute of Information & Communication Technology,

3. Dr. Akshai Aggarwal, Vice-Chancellor, Gujarat Technological University,

4. Dr. P. L. Salinkar, Alumni, Indian Institute of Technology, Mumbai,

5. Dr. Ajit Kumar, Professor, Institute of Chemical Technology, Mumbai,

Chanchal Dass, FIE, Email: cdass01@gmail.com, Mobile: +91-8320172787

Gratitude

I have to devote a large portion of my time throughout my life on my research projects and as a consequence of that I could not perform many of the duties related to my family, parenting, social, and many others. I feel privileged and lucky to have my wife Bela. She has taken all the pain for taking up additional responsibilities to maintain our family in a healthy and organised manner. I convey my sincere gratitude to her.

I have to face many ups and downs in my career path and got many supports, encouragements, and motivation to keep myself floating. Among many others, I wish to convey my sincere gratitude who had special impact in my life:

1. Sri Kamal Das

2. Sri Gopinath Manna

3. Sri Badal Roy

4. Sri Asim Ganguly

5. Sri Kamaleshwar Rai

6. Sri Mahesh Krovvidi

7. Dr. Ranadhir Mukhopadhyaya

8. Dr. Asim Banerjee

9. Dr. P. L. Salinkar

From Author to Readers

Why am I writing this book?

The authors write a book with some objectives in their mind and readers read a book with some objectives in mind. For an effective process of reading and writing a book, both the objectives of writing a book and the objectives of reading a book should match. For this purpose, I am writing my objectives of writing this book here so that the readers can know the objectives of writing this book clearly and can match them with their own objectives of reading this book beforehand before starting to read this book.

Mathematics is often seen as a collection of problems to be solved, a series of challenges that test our ability to apply formulas and algorithms. However, this perception can overshadow the true beauty of the subject—the concepts that form the foundation of all mathematical reasoning. In writing this book, Vector Algebra, my primary objective is to shift the focus from problem-solving to a deep, conceptual understanding of mathematics.

As someone who has spent many years both learning and teaching mathematics, I have seen firsthand how students can struggle when they are not given the opportunity to fully grasp the concepts before being asked to solve problems. This struggle is not a reflection of their abilities but rather of the way mathematics is often taught. With this book, I aim to change that approach.

My goal is to present each concept in vector algebra clearly and thoroughly, without rushing into complex problem-solving. I believe that by understanding the "why" behind each concept, students will be better equipped to handle the "how" when it comes time to apply their knowledge. This book is structured to guide you through each topic, one step at a time, allowing you to build a solid foundation before moving on to more advanced ideas.

In addition to focusing on conceptual understanding, I have also included sections on geometric modeling and animation using MS Excel. These tools are designed to help you visualize the concepts, making them easier to understand and more relevant to real-world applications. In today's technologically advanced world, it is essential that we use all available resources to make learning more effective and engaging.

Whether you are a student, teacher, or self-learner, I hope this book will serve as a valuable resource in your mathematical journey. My intention is not just to help you pass exams or complete assignments but to foster a true appreciation for the elegance and power of vector algebra.

Thank you for choosing to embark on this journey with me. I hope you find this book both informative and inspiring, and that it helps you see mathematics in a new light.

Warm regards,

Chanchal Dass 15th August, 2024

Summary of Chapters

This book, Vector Algebra, is designed to guide readers through the fundamental concepts of vector algebra, emphasizing a deep understanding of each topic without the immediate pressure of problem-solving. There are five chapters in this book. Below is a summary of the chapters:

1. **Chapter 1: Introduction to Vector Algebra**
   This chapter lays the groundwork for the study of vector algebra. It introduces the basic definition of vectors, their properties, and their importance in both two-dimensional and three-dimensional spaces. Readers will learn about different types of vectors, including zero vectors, unit vectors, and co-initial vectors, and will begin to understand the significance of vector operations.

2. **Chapter 2: Vector Operations**
   Building on the introduction, this chapter delves into the operations that can be performed with vectors. It covers vector addition, scalar multiplication, and the geometric interpretation of these operations. The chapter also introduces the concept of direction cosines and how they relate to the orientation of vectors in space.

3. **Chapter 3: Dot and Cross Products**
   This chapter focuses on two fundamental vector operations: the dot product and the cross product. It explains how these operations are performed, their geometric interpretations, and their applications in various fields, such as physics and engineering. The chapter also discusses the projection of vectors and how to calculate the angle between two vectors.

4. **Chapter 4: Vectors in Three-Dimension**

In this chapter, the application of vector algebra to three dimensions is explored in detail. Topics include the vector equations of lines and planes, the shortest distance between two lines, and the concept of coplanarity. This chapter also introduces the concept of the scalar triple product and its significance in calculating volumes of parallelepipeds.

5. **Chapter 5: Geometric Modeling and Animation Using MS Excel**

   This chapter is a unique feature of the book, designed to enhance the reader's understanding of vector concepts through visualization. It provides step-by-step instructions on how to use MS Excel for geometric modeling and animation, making abstract concepts more tangible and easier to grasp. The tools presented in this chapter are intended to foster self-discovery and deepen the reader's conceptual understanding.

Each chapter is crafted to build upon the last, ensuring that readers develop a solid and cohesive understanding of vector algebra. By the end of the book, readers will not only have a strong grasp of the theoretical concepts but will also be able to visualize and apply these concepts in practical scenarios.

List of Institutions

List of institutions and universities where mathematics workshops/lectures were conducted:

1. National Institute of Oceanography, Goa, for research scholars.

2. Gujarat Technological University, Gujarat, for engineering college faculties as well as students (Around 20 Math Workshops).

3. Sahajanand Laser Technologies Limited, Gujarat, for practicing professionals.

4. Dhirubhai Ambani Institute of Information and Communication Technology, Gujarat, (3 Workshops) for Higher Secondary, B. Tech., M. Tech., and Ph. D. students.

5. Sri Padmavati Mahila Mahavidyalaya, Tirupati, for B. Sc. and M. Sc. (Maths) students.

6. Ganpat University, Gujarat, for B. Sc. (Maths) and M. Sc. (Maths) students.

7. eInfochips Training and Research Academy, Gujarat, for M. Tech. students.

8. Silver Oak College, Gujarat, for engineering students and faculties.

9. Venus International College, Gujarat, for B. Tech. students.

10. Gujarat University, Gujarat, for engineering college faculties from universities (RUSA sponsored workshop).

11. Indian Institute of Technology, Gandhinagar, for Ph. D. (Math) students.

12. Shri Swaminarayan Institute of Technology, Gandhinagar, for B. Tech. and M. Sc. students.

13. Kadi Sarva Vishwavidyalaya, Gandhinagar, B. Sc., M. Sc. students and university faculties.

14. Parul University, Vadodara, for university mathematics faculties.

15. Pandit Deendayal Petroleum University, Gandhinagar, for MBA students.

16. St. Xavier's College, Ahmedabad, for B. Sc. and M. Sc. (Maths) students.

17. University of Dhaka, for PG students and scientists.

18. Rayat Bahra University, Punjab, for faculties.

19. Chandigarh University, Punjab, for faculties.

20. Hotel Grande Delmon, Goa, for class ten to doctoral students and faculties.

21. I. K. Gujral Punjab Technical University, Punjab, for faculties.

22. Central University of Kashmir, Srinagar, for B. Sc. and M. Sc. math students.

23. University of Kashmir, Srinagar, for research scholars and mathematics faculties.

24. State Council for Educational Research and Training, Government of Goa, for school teachers.

25. Institution of Engineers, Maharashtra, State Centre, Mumbai, 2 workshops, open to all.

26. College of Engineering, Pune, Maharashtra, for university faculties and doctoral students.

27. Goa University, Panaji, Goa, open to all.

28. Institute of Chemical Technology, Mumbai, for students and faculties.

29. Indian Institute of Technology, Kanpur, for UG, PG and doctoral students.

30. Tribhuvan University, Nepal, for faculties and doctoral students.

31. Adani Institute of Infrastructure Technology, Ahmedabad, for UG students.

32. Indian Institute of Technology, Mumbai, for UG, PG and doctoral students.

33. Indian Institute of Technology, Kharagpur, IMS conference.

34. Indian Institute of Science and Educational Research, Pune, Time conference.

35. ICAPAM, Hotel Hilton, Dubai.

Chapter 1

Introduction to Vector Algebra

I learned my early class mathematics from the books of Keshab Chandra Nag. All his books are wonderfully written and very popular among the students to date. I could learn each and every topic easily. However, when I reached higher classes, I started facing problems in understanding advanced mathematical concepts. Somehow I completed my studies and was very successful in my professional career. However, I always tried to find the reasons for facing the difficulties in understanding advanced mathematical concepts. I have realized that my basic mathematics skills are not that weak still I have faced problems in understanding higher mathematics. So, at the age of 55 years, I left my job and started research on making mathematics learning easy and enjoyable.

I have realized that one of the reasons for my poor understanding of higher mathematics was that all the mathematics I learned without any understanding of why I am learning it.

So, I feel that if someone learns mathematics based on the reasoning on why he is learning that then this difficulty in understanding higher mathematical concepts will not arise.

With this thought in mind, I am writing this mathematics book "An Introduction to Vector Algebra."

I have analyzed all the mathematics that is being taught from Class 1 to Class 12 in NCERT books. Around 30 broad topics or ideas are being taught in those 12 classes with a total number of chapters are 188. So, on average, each topic takes 6 chapters. But to my surprise, I saw that the number system topic has covered around 53 chapters spanning from class 1 to class 11. The number of total chapters in each class along with the chapters on numbers are given in table-1 and shown in Figure-1.

1.1   No of chapters in class 1 to 12 of CBSE Board

The class-wise chapters are given below for reference:

Table 1.1: Total chapters in Class 1 to 12 = 188

Class	Total Chapters
1	13 CHAPTERS
2	15 CHAPTERS
3	14 CHAPTERS
4	14 CHAPTERS
5	14 CHAPTERS
6	14 CHAPTERS
7	15 CHAPTERS
8	16 CHAPTERS
9	17 CHAPTERS
10	17 CHAPTERS
11	18 CHAPTERS
12	21 CHAPTERS

The number of chapters in Vector Algebra is given below:

Table 1.2: NCERT Math Book: Total Chapters and Chapters on Vector Algebra

Class	Total Chapter	Chapters On Vector Algebra
1	13	0
2	15	0
3	14	0
4	14	0
5	14	0
6	14	0
7	15	0
8	16	0
9	17	0
10	17	0
11	18	0
12	21	1

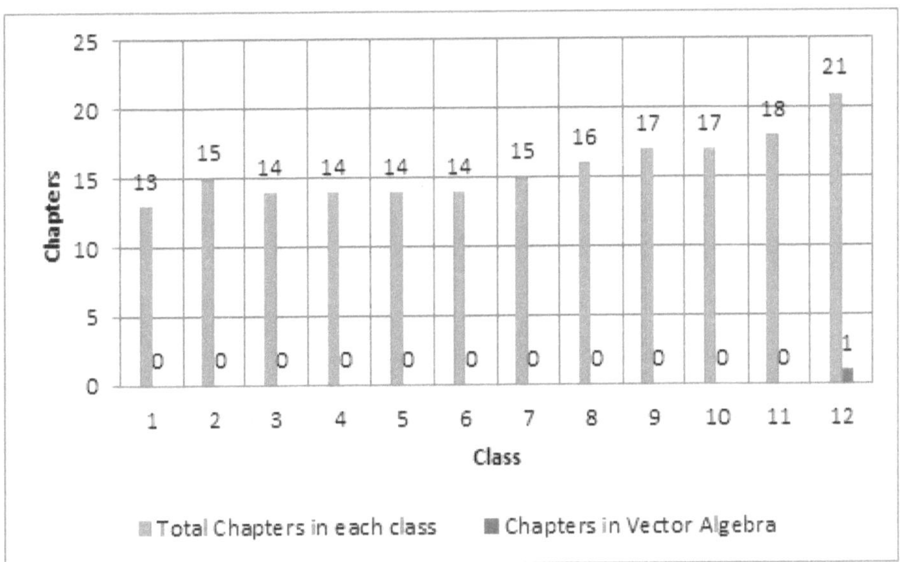

Table 1.3: Class-12: Vector Algebra chapters in NCERT books

Class	Chapter No	Chapter Name	Page
12	10	Vector Algebra	424

It can be seen that there is only one chapter in the entire mathematics syllabus. The 10th Chapter of class-XII NCERT book deals with vector algebra.

There is another chapter in the class-XII NCERT math book which deals with "Three-dimensional Geometry". This is chapter 11. Many of the concepts of three-dimensional geometry have been explained with the help of vector algebra. In one way we can say that Chapter 11 is the application of the vectors in three-dimensional space that we learned in Chapter 10. For completeness, I will include both chapters in this book.

Chapter 2

Why We Require Vector Algebra

Many times in real-life situations, we are required to express some quantities that have both magnitude and direction. Vectors are a very effective tool to represent quantities that have both magnitude and direction. Geometrically, the vector is a directed line segment as shown in the figure below:

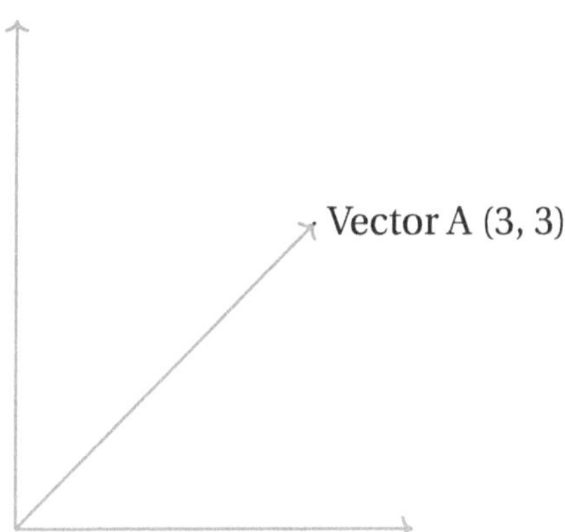

Figure 2.1: Geometrical representation of a vector

Mathematically a vector is represented by 2 elements like (2, 3) in 2D, by 3 elements like (2,5,3) in 3D, and by n elements in n dimension.

So, we can visualize the two and three-dimensional vectors and the results of their binary operations. But, when the vectors contain more than three elements, then visualizing these vectors is difficult. However, the majority of the thoughts that are applicable to two and three dimensions are equally applicable in higher dimensions. So, it is very important to understand the vector algebra concepts in two and three dimensions.

In earlier days, there was no technology available for modeling and animations. For this reason, we were required to write every mathematical concept in a descriptive way. Students were required to learn the mathematical concepts from these descriptive explanations. It is slow and a intuitive learning process. Nowadays we are in a technological age and we can easily create any geometrical model and animate it.

For this purpose, we have included one chapter on geometric modeling and animation in MS Excel to facilitate the learners to model and animate every vector algebra concept while reading for clear understanding. It will help them understand all the concepts easily and put them in self-learning and self-discovery mode. These geometrical modeling and animation tools also help them in modeling any real-life problem related to any field.

I have used MS Excel for modeling and animation because it does not require any coding or programming knowledge for modeling and animation.

Chapter 3

What is vector?

As mentioned in chapter 1, there is only one chapter on vector algebra in CBSE syllabus as shown below:

Table 3.1: Class-12: Vector Algebra chapters in NCERT books

Class	Chapter No	Chapter Name	Page
12	10	Vector Algebra	424

There is another chapter titled THREE DIMENTIONAL GEOME-TRY. This is chapter 11 of class 12 as given in table 3.2.

Table 3.2: Class-12: Vector Algebra chapters in NCERT books

Class	Chapter No	Chapter Name	Page
12	11	Three Dimensional Geometry	462

In this chapter, we will cover the basic concepts of Vector algebra and in the later chapter, we will cover the use of these vector algebra concepts in three-dimensional space.

3.1   What is Vector?

A *vector* is a quantity that has both magnitude and direction.

Directed Line Segment: A *directed line segment* has magnitude and direction. Hence, geometrically, any vector can be represented as a directed line segment.

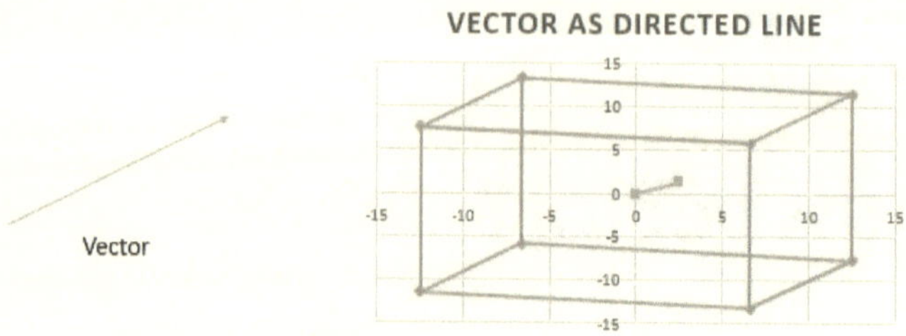

Figure 3.1: A vector as a directed line.

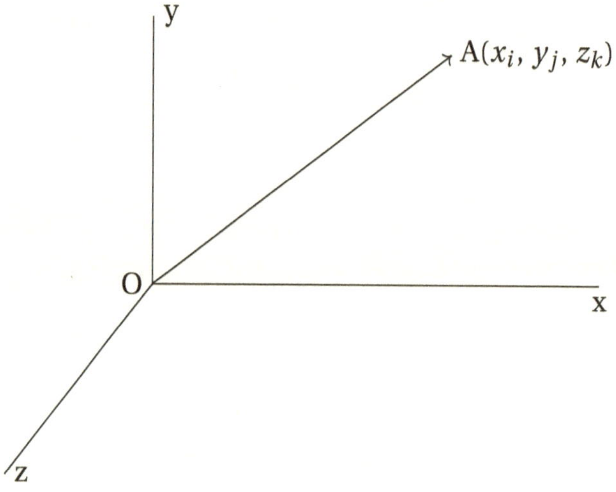

Figure 3.2: A vector OA in 3D space

Vector is represented by a group of ordered numbers (x, y), (x, y, z).

Some of the properties of Vectors are given below:

1. Initial Point: The point O from where the vector starts as shown in the figure given above.

2. Terminal Point: The point A where it ends

3. Magnitude: The distance between the initial and terminals of a vector such as d.

4. Direction: The arrow indicates the direction of the vector such as t.

3.2   Type of Vectors

- **Zero vector:** A vector whose initial and terminal points coincide.

- **Unit vector:** A vector whose magnitude is unity (i.e.,1 unit).

- **Co-initial vectors:** Vectors having same initial point.

- **Collinear Vectors:** Vectors which are parallel to the same line.

- **Equal Vectors:** Vectors having same magnitude and direction.

- **Free Vectors:** The vectors defined above are such that any of them may be subject to its parallel displacement without changing their magnitude and direction. Such vectors are called free vectors. Throughout this chapter, we will be dealing with free vectors only.

Chapter 4

Vector operations

4.1   Vector addition

Vector Addition is a fundamental operation in vector algebra where two or more vectors are combined to form a new vector, called the resultant vector.

Definition

Given two vectors **A** and **B**, the vector sum or resultant vector **R** is obtained by placing the tail of **B** at the head of **A**. The vector **R** is then drawn from the tail of **A** to the head of **B**.

Mathematical Representation

If **A** has components A_x and A_y in a 2D plane, and **B** has components B_x and B_y, then the resultant vector **R** will have components:

$$\mathbf{R} = \mathbf{A} + \mathbf{B} = (A_x + B_x)\mathbf{i} + (A_y + B_y)\mathbf{j}$$

In 3D, with components A_z and B_z, the resultant is:

$$\mathbf{R} = (A_x + B_x)\mathbf{i} + (A_y + B_y)\mathbf{j} + (A_z + B_z)\mathbf{k}$$

Geometric Representation

- **Triangle Law of Vector Addition**: Place vector **B** at the end of vector **A**. The resultant vector **R** is drawn from the start of **A** to the end of **B**.

- **Parallelogram Law of Vector Addition**: Place vectors **A** and **B** so that they start from the same point. The resultant vector **R** is the diagonal of the parallelogram formed by **A** and **B**.

Example

If $\mathbf{A} = 3\mathbf{i} + 2\mathbf{j}$ and $\mathbf{B} = 1\mathbf{i} + 4\mathbf{j}$, then:

$$\mathbf{R} = (3 + 1)\mathbf{i} + (2 + 4)\mathbf{j} = 4\mathbf{i} + 6\mathbf{j}$$

So, the resultant vector **R** has components $4\mathbf{i}$ and $6\mathbf{j}$.

Properties

- **Commutative Property**: $\mathbf{A} + \mathbf{B} = \mathbf{B} + \mathbf{A}$

- **Associative Property**: $\mathbf{A} + (\mathbf{B} + \mathbf{C}) = (\mathbf{A} + \mathbf{B}) + \mathbf{C}$

Vector addition is essential in physics and engineering, where it is used to combine forces, velocities, and other vector quantities.

Geometric Representation

The geometric interpretation of triangular law and parallelogram law is shown below:

1. **Triangle law of vector addition:** For vector addition, place the initial point of one vector to the terminal point of the other. It is known as the *triangle law of vector addition.*

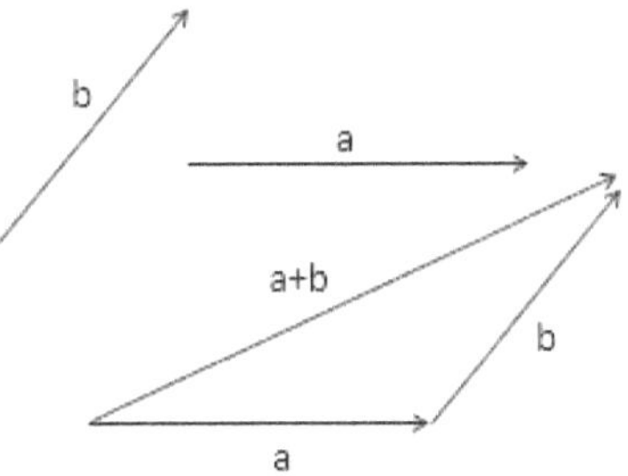

Figure 4.1: Triangle law of vector addition.

2. **Parallelogram law of vector addition:** For vector addition indexVector addition, place the initial points of both the vectors and complete the parallelogram. The diagonal represents the *resultant vector.*

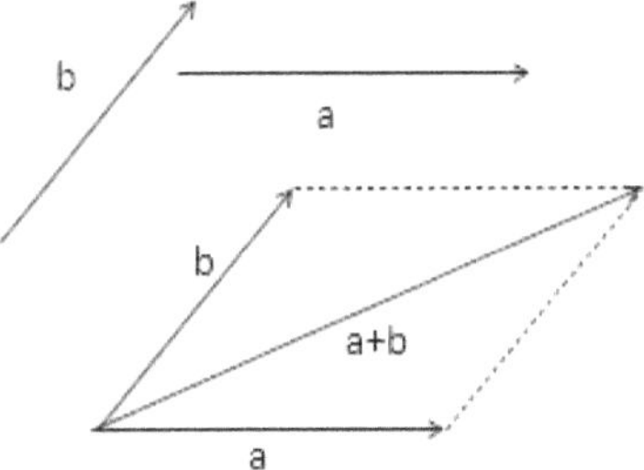

Figure 4.2: Parallelogram law of vector addition.

4.2 Multiplication of a Vector by a Scalar

Multiplication of a Vector by a Scalar is an operation where a vector is multiplied by a scalar (a real number). The result is a new vector that is in the same direction as the original vector but scaled in magnitude by the scalar value.

Definition

Given a vector $\mathbf{A} = A_x\mathbf{i} + A_y\mathbf{j} + A_z\mathbf{k}$ and a scalar k, the multiplication of the vector $\mathbf{A}$ by the scalar k is defined as:

$$\mathbf{B} = k\mathbf{A} = k(A_x\mathbf{i} + A_y\mathbf{j} + A_z\mathbf{k}) = (kA_x)\mathbf{i} + (kA_y)\mathbf{j} + (kA_z)\mathbf{k}$$

Here, $\mathbf{B}$ is the new vector, and its components are obtained by multiplying each component of the original vector $\mathbf{A}$ by the scalar k.

Geometric Interpretation

- If $k > 1$, the vector $\mathbf{B}$ is stretched in the same direction as $\mathbf{A}$. - If $0 < k < 1$, the vector $\mathbf{B}$ is shortened in the same direction as $\mathbf{A}$. - If $k = 0$, the result is the zero vector $\mathbf{0}$. - If $k < 0$, the vector $\mathbf{B}$ is reversed in direction (pointing in the opposite direction to $\mathbf{A}$) and scaled by $|k|$.

Example

Let $\mathbf{A} = 2\mathbf{i} + 3\mathbf{j} - \mathbf{k}$ and $k = 4$. The scalar multiplication is:

$$\mathbf{B} = 4\mathbf{A} = 4(2\mathbf{i} + 3\mathbf{j} - \mathbf{k}) = 8\mathbf{i} + 12\mathbf{j} - 4\mathbf{k}$$

So, the new vector $\mathbf{B}$ has components $8\mathbf{i}$, $12\mathbf{j}$, and $-4\mathbf{k}$.

Properties

- **Distributive Property:** $k(\mathbf{A} + \mathbf{B}) = k\mathbf{A} + k\mathbf{B}$

- **Associative Property:** $(k_1 k_2)\mathbf{A} = k_1(k_2\mathbf{A})$

- **Multiplication by 1:** $1\mathbf{A} = \mathbf{A}$

- **Multiplication by 0:** $0\mathbf{A} = \mathbf{0}$

Multiplication of a vector by a scalar is fundamental in vector algebra, particularly in scaling vectors, defining vector spaces, and understanding vector fields.

4.3 Geometric Interpretation of Multiplication of a Vector and Scalar

$Definition needed Multiplication of a Vector by a Scalar$

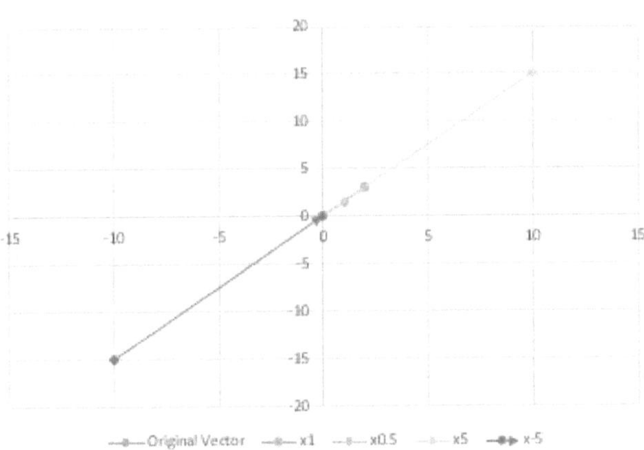

Figure 4.3: Scalar multiplication of a vector.

4.4 Components of a Vector in 2D and 3D

4.4.1 Components of a Vector in 2D

A vector in 2D space can be expressed in terms of its components along the x- and y-axes. If **A** is a vector in 2D, its component form is:

$$\mathbf{A} = A_x\mathbf{i} + A_y\mathbf{j}$$

Where:

- A_x is the scalar component of **A** along the x-axis.
- A_y is the scalar component of **A** along the y-axis.
- **i** and **j** are the unit vectors along the x- and y-axes, respectively.

Example: Consider the vector $\mathbf{A} = 5\mathbf{i} + 7\mathbf{j}$. Here:

- The component along the x-axis is $A_x = 5$.
- The component along the y-axis is $A_y = 7$.
- The vector **A** can be represented as $(5, 7)$ in component form.

4.4.2 Components of a Vector in 3D

A vector in 3D space can be expressed in terms of its components along the x-, y-, and z-axes. If **A** is a vector in 3D, its component form is:

$$\mathbf{A} = A_x\mathbf{i} + A_y\mathbf{j} + A_z\mathbf{k}$$

Where:

- A_x is the scalar component of **A** along the x-axis.
- A_y is the scalar component of **A** along the y-axis.
- A_z is the scalar component of **A** along the z-axis.
- **i**, **j**, and **k** are the unit vectors along the x-, y-, and z-axes, respectively.

Example: Consider the vector $\mathbf{A} = 3\mathbf{i} - 4\mathbf{j} + 2\mathbf{k}$. Here:

- The component along the x-axis is $A_x = 3$.

- The component along the y-axis is $A_y = -4$.

- The component along the z-axis is $A_z = 2$.

- The vector $\mathbf{A}$ can be represented as $(3, -4, 2)$ in component form.

General Form of Vector Components

The general form of a vector's components in 2D and 3D can be represented as:

- **2D:** $\mathbf{A} = A_x\mathbf{i} + A_y\mathbf{j}$

- **3D:** $\mathbf{A} = A_x\mathbf{i} + A_y\mathbf{j} + A_z\mathbf{k}$

These components allow the vector to be broken down into its effects in each of the coordinate directions, which is crucial for performing operations like addition, subtraction, and dot products in vector algebra.

Vector $\overrightarrow{OP} = [7, 5, 6]$

Components of vector $\overrightarrow{OP}$:
$$x\text{-component} = [7, 0, 0]$$
$$y\text{-component} = [0, 5, 0]$$
$$z\text{-component} = [0, 0, 6]$$
$$|OP| = \sqrt{7^2 + 5^2 + 6^2} = 10.488$$

The figure for the above vector is shown in fig. 4.4.

Chanchal Dass, FIE, Email: cdass01@gmail.com, Mobile: +91-8320172787

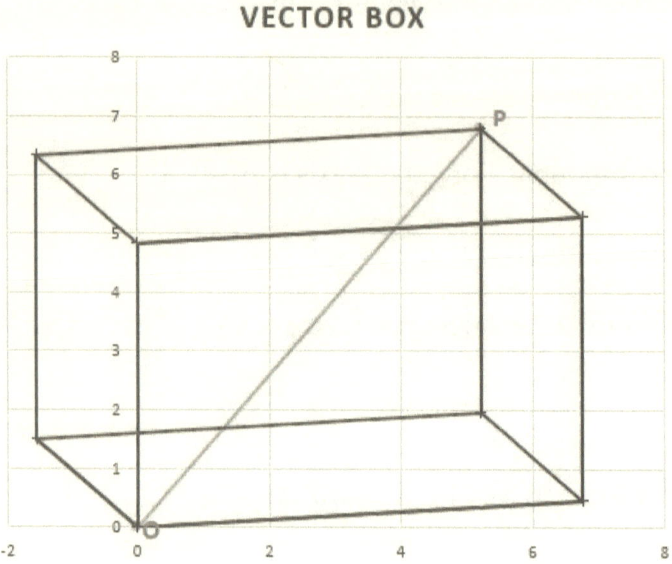

Figure 4.4: Components of $\overrightarrow{OP}$

4.4.2.1   Vector Joining Two Points

4.5   Vector Joining Two Points

In vector algebra, one of the fundamental concepts is the idea of a vector that connects or joins two points in space. This vector, often referred to as the position vector, provides a way to describe the direction and distance between two points in either two-dimensional (2D) or three-dimensional (3D) space.

Definition

Given two points $P(x_1, y_1, z_1)$ and $Q(x_2, y_2, z_2)$ in space, the vector **PQ** that joins these points is defined as:

$$\mathbf{PQ} = (x_2 - x_1)\mathbf{i} + (y_2 - y_1)\mathbf{j} + (z_2 - z_1)\mathbf{k}$$

Where:

- (x_1, y_1, z_1) are the coordinates of point P.

- (x_2, y_2, z_2) are the coordinates of point Q.

- $\mathbf{i}$, $\mathbf{j}$, and $\mathbf{k}$ are the unit vectors along the x-, y-, and z-axes, respectively.

2D Space

In 2D space, if the points $P(x_1, y_1)$ and $Q(x_2, y_2)$ are given, the vector joining these two points is:

$$\mathbf{PQ} = (x_2 - x_1)\mathbf{i} + (y_2 - y_1)\mathbf{j}$$

This vector provides both the direction and magnitude of the line segment from point P to point Q in a two-dimensional plane.

3D Space

In 3D space, the vector joining the points $P(x_1, y_1, z_1)$ and $Q(x_2, y_2, z_2)$ is:

$$\mathbf{PQ} = (x_2 - x_1)\mathbf{i} + (y_2 - y_1)\mathbf{j} + (z_2 - z_1)\mathbf{k}$$

This vector represents the direction and distance from P to Q in three-dimensional space, accounting for the changes in the x-, y-, and z-coordinates.

Example in 2D

Let $P(1, 2)$ and $Q(4, 6)$. The vector joining these two points is:

$$\mathbf{PQ} = (4 - 1)\mathbf{i} + (6 - 2)\mathbf{j} = 3\mathbf{i} + 4\mathbf{j}$$

Example in 3D

Let $P(1, 2, 3)$ and $Q(4, 6, 8)$. The vector joining these two points is:

$$\mathbf{PQ} = (4 - 1)\mathbf{i} + (6 - 2)\mathbf{j} + (8 - 3)\mathbf{k} = 3\mathbf{i} + 4\mathbf{j} + 5\mathbf{k}$$

Applications

Understanding the vector joining two points is crucial in various fields such as physics, engineering, and computer graphics. It is used to determine distances, and directions, and in performing operations like vector addition and subtraction.

Let the two points be P $[x_1, y_1, z_1]$ and Q $[x_2, y_2, z_2]$.

$$PQ = Q - P = [x_2 - x_1, \; y_2 - y_1, \; z_2 - z_1]$$
$$|PQ| = \sqrt{(x_2 - x_1)^2 + (y_2 - y_1)^2 + (z_2 - z_1)^2}$$

4.6   Section Formula

A "ratio" is just a comparison between two different things.

Suppose there are thirty-five people, fifteen of whom are men. Then the ratio of men to women is 15 to 20 (expressed as $15 : 20$).

In mathematics, two variables are proportional if a change in one is always accompanied by a change in the other, and if the changes are always related by use of a constant multiplier. The constant is called the *coefficient of proportionality* or *proportionality constant*.

The *section formula* tells us the coordinates of the point that divides a given line segment into two parts such that their lengths are in the ratio $m : n$, as shown in fig. 4.5.

Figure 4.5: Ratio of two line segments.

$$x = \frac{(mx_2 + nx_1)}{(m + n)}$$

$$y = \frac{(my_2 + ny_1)}{(m + n)}$$

If P $[x_1, y_1, z_1]$ and Q $[x_2, y_2, z_2]$ are two given points, then

Chanchal Dass, FIE, Email: cdass01@gmail.com, Mobile: +91-8320172787

1. $R_{in}=[x, y]$ divides PQ in the ratio $m : n$ INTERNALLY

$$x = \frac{(mx_2 + nx_1)}{(m+n)}$$

$$y = \frac{(my_2 + ny_1)}{(m+n)}$$

2. $R_{out}=[x, y]$ divides PQ in the ratio $m : n$ EXTERNALLY

$$x = \frac{(mx_2 - nx_1)}{(m-n)}$$

$$y = \frac{(my_2 - ny_1)}{(m-n)}$$

General rule:

1. **Internally** $(m : n)$**:** Calculate the distance (L) between the points.

$$x = m\frac{L}{(m+n)}, \; y = n\frac{L}{(m+n)}$$

2. **Externally** $(m : n)$**:** Calculate the distance (L) between the points.

$$x = m\frac{L}{(m-n)}, \; y = n\frac{L}{(m-n)}$$

Example: Consider two points P and Q with position vector $\overrightarrow{OP} = 3a - 2b$ and $\overrightarrow{OQ} = a + b$. Find the position vector of a point R which divides the line segment joining P and Q in the ratio $2 : 1$

1. internally, and

2. externally

Answer:

1. Internally,

$$x = \frac{2(a+b) + 1(3a-2b)}{(2+1)} = \frac{5a}{3}$$

2. Externally,

$$x = \frac{2(a+b) - 1(3a-2b)(2-1)}{2-1} = 4b - a$$

4.6.1 Section Formula for Vectors (Internally)

$$\vec{V_1} = (0\hat{i} + 3\hat{j})$$

$$\vec{V_2} = (8\hat{i} + 3\hat{j})$$

A vector divides them internally in the ratio 3:1

$$\vec{r} = \frac{m\vec{V_2} + n\vec{V_1}}{m+n}$$
$$= \frac{3(8\hat{i} + 3\hat{j}) + 1((0\hat{i} + 3\hat{j}))}{3+1}$$
$$= \frac{(24\hat{i} + 9\hat{j} + 0\hat{i} + 3\hat{j})}{4}$$
$$= \frac{(24\hat{i} + 12\hat{j})}{4}$$
$$= (6\hat{i} + 3\hat{j})$$

4.6.2 Section Formula for Vector (Externally)

$$\vec{V_1} = (0\hat{i} + 3\hat{j})$$

$$\vec{V_2} = (8\hat{i} + 3\hat{j})$$

A vector divides them externally in the ratio 3:1

$$\vec{r} = \frac{m\vec{V_2} - n\vec{V_1}}{m-n}$$
$$= \frac{3(8\hat{i} + 3\hat{j}) - 1((0\hat{i} + 3\hat{j}))}{3-1}$$
$$= \frac{(24\hat{i} + 9\hat{j} - 0\hat{i} - 3\hat{j})}{2}$$
$$= \frac{(24\hat{i} + 6\hat{j})}{2}$$
$$= (12\hat{i} + 3\hat{j}$$

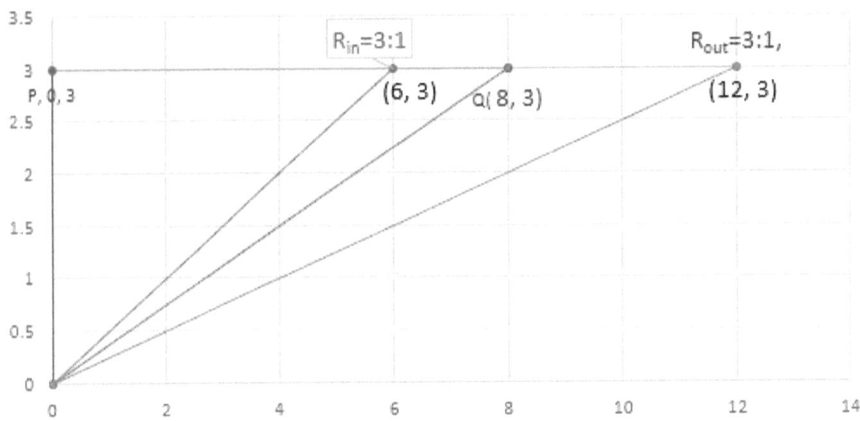

Figure 4.6: Internal and external ratio of line segments.

4.7 Direction Cosines

In vector algebra, the orientation of a vector in three-dimensional space is described by the angles it makes with the coordinate axes. The cosines of these angles are known as **Direction Cosines**. They are essential for understanding the vector's direction relative to the coordinate system.

4.7.1 Definition

Let **A** be a vector in 3D space with components A_x, A_y, and A_z along the x-, y-, and z-axes, respectively. The direction cosines of the vector **A** are the cosines of the angles α, β, and γ that the vector makes with the x-, y-, and z-axes, respectively. They are denoted by l, m, and n, and are defined as:

$$l = \cos\alpha = \frac{A_x}{|\mathbf{A}|}, \quad m = \cos\beta = \frac{A_y}{|\mathbf{A}|}, \quad n = \cos\gamma = \frac{A_z}{|\mathbf{A}|}$$

Where $|\mathbf{A}|$ is the magnitude of the vector **A**:

$$|\mathbf{A}| = \sqrt{A_x^2 + A_y^2 + A_z^2}$$

4.7.2 Properties of Direction Cosines

The direction cosines l, m, and n have the following properties:

- The sum of the squares of the direction cosines is always equal to 1:

$$l^2 + m^2 + n^2 = 1$$

- Direction cosines uniquely determine the direction of the vector in space.

- They are useful in converting between vector representations and in finding the angle between vectors.

4.7.3 Example-1

Consider a vector $\mathbf{A} = 3\mathbf{i} + 4\mathbf{j} + 5\mathbf{k}$. The magnitude of the vector is:

$$|\mathbf{A}| = \sqrt{3^2 + 4^2 + 5^2} = \sqrt{9 + 16 + 25} = \sqrt{50} = 5\sqrt{2}$$

The direction cosines of $\mathbf{A}$ are:

$$l = \frac{3}{5\sqrt{2}}, \quad m = \frac{4}{5\sqrt{2}}, \quad n = \frac{5}{5\sqrt{2}}$$

4.7.4 Application

Direction cosines are widely used in physics, engineering, and computer graphics to describe the orientation of vectors, particularly in three-dimensional space. They are also essential in solving problems involving angles between vectors, projection of vectors, and determining the direction of a vector in space.

4.7.5 Example-2

Vector $\overrightarrow{OP} = [7, 5, 6]$
Components of vector $\overrightarrow{OP}$:
$$\text{x-component} = [7, 0, 0]$$

$$y\text{-component} = [0,\, 5,\, 0]$$
$$z\text{-component} = [0,\, 0,\, 6]$$
$$r = |OP| = \sqrt{7^2 + 5^2 + 6^2} = 10.488$$

$$l = \cos(\alpha) = \frac{x}{r} = \frac{7}{10.488}$$
$$m = \cos(\beta) = \frac{y}{r} = \frac{5}{10.488}$$
$$n = \cos(\gamma) = \frac{z}{r} = \frac{6}{10.488}$$

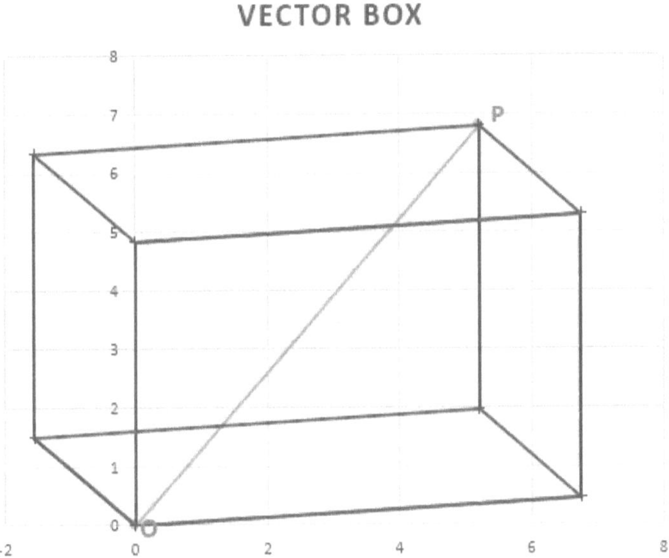

Figure 4.7: Vector Box representation in 3D

Direction ratios:

a=l r, b=m r, c=n r (r=-n to n)

vector box

0.840052	1.073864	0.96176	Radian
48.13146	61.52787	55.10477	Degree

Chanchal Dass, FIE, Email: cdass01@gmail.com, Mobile: +91-8320172787

4.8   Summary of Vector parameters

- Vector is a directed line segment.
- Vector has both Magnitude and Direction
- Vector is represented by a group of ordered numbers (x,y), (x,y,z)

Properties of Vectors:

1. Initial Point: o

2. Terminal Point: A

3. Magnitude: d

4. Direction, t

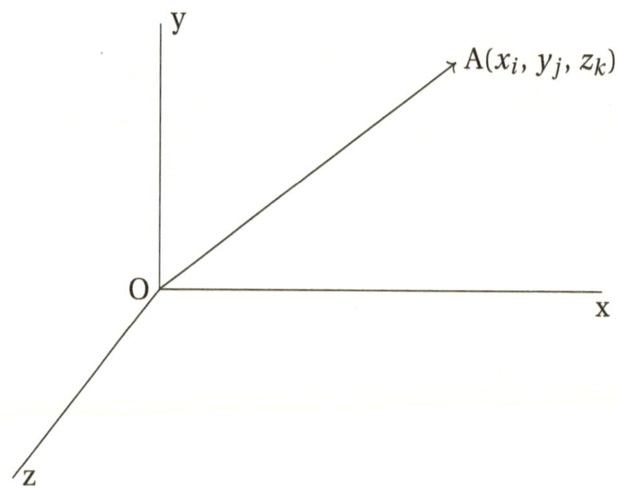

Figure 4.8: Representation of 3D vector

4.9   Vector representations

Vector Representation: $A = (A_x i, A_y j, A_z k)$

(Ax, Ay, Az   are scalars)

4.10   The magnitude or Absolute Value of A

:

The magnitude or Absolute Value of a vector A is: $\sqrt{(A_x^2 + A_y^2 + A_z^2)}$
Example: **F=3i+4j-12k**
$F^2 = (3)^2 + (4)^2 + (12)^2$ F =13N

4.11   Graphical Representation of Vectors

Two vectors are shown below for reference:

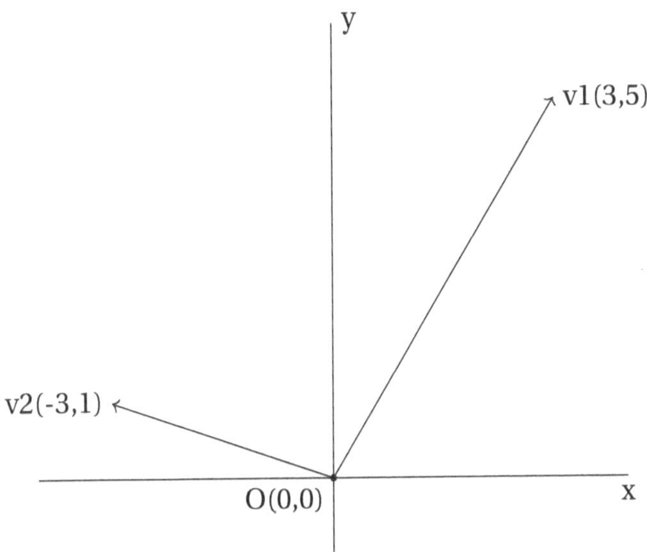

Figure 4.9: 2D Vectors

The following point shows the major issues that students face while studying vector algebra:

- Vectors are represented by (x, y) in 2d and (x, y, z) in 3d

- Vectors has an initial point represented by (x1,y1) or (x1,y1,z1) and end point (x2,y2) or (x2,y2,z2).

- Then how the vectors represented by (x,y) or (x,y,z)

4.12   Representation of Vectors in 2D and 3D

In vector algebra, vectors are geometric entities that have both magnitude and direction. They can be represented in either two-dimensional (2D) or three-dimensional (3D) space.

4.12.1   Vectors in 2D

A vector in 2D space is represented by its components along the x- and y-axes. If **A** is a vector in 2D, it can be written as:

$$\mathbf{A} = (x, y)$$

Where:

- x is the component of the vector along the x-axis.

- y is the component of the vector along the y-axis.

4.12.2   Vectors in 3D

A vector in 3D space is represented by its components along the x-, y-, and z-axes. If **B** is a vector in 3D, it can be written as:

$$\mathbf{B} = (x, y, z)$$

Where:

- x is the component of the vector along the x-axis.

- y is the component of the vector along the y-axis.

- z is the component of the vector along the z-axis.

4.12.3 Initial and End Points of a Vector

A vector is often defined by its initial point (also known as the tail) and its end point (also known as the head).

In 2D:

- The initial point is represented by (x_1, y_1).

- The end point is represented by (x_2, y_2).

The vector **A** joining these two points can be expressed as:

$$\mathbf{A} = (x_2 - x_1, y_2 - y_1)$$

In 3D:

- The initial point is represented by (x_1, y_1, z_1).

- The end point is represented by (x_2, y_2, z_2).

The vector **B** joining these two points can be expressed as:

$$\mathbf{B} = (x_2 - x_1, y_2 - y_1, z_2 - z_1)$$

4.12.4 Example in 2D

Consider the initial point $P(1,2)$ and the end point $Q(4,5)$. The vector **PQ** is:

$$\mathbf{PQ} = (4 - 1, 5 - 2) = (3, 3)$$

Example in 3D

Consider the initial point $P(1,2,3)$ and the end point $Q(4,5,6)$. The vector **PQ** is:

$$\mathbf{PQ} = (4 - 1, 5 - 2, 6 - 3) = (3, 3, 3)$$

This vector represents the direction and distance from point P to point Q in 3D space.

Example:

The initial point A=(1, 2), and, end point B=(5,4).

What is the vector AB?
Answer: The given vector is (5-1), (4-2)) =(4,2)
The given vectors are shown below:

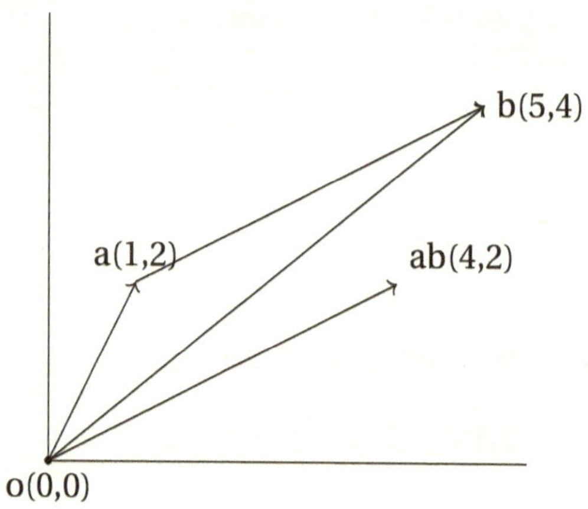

Figure 4.10: Vector ab

4.12.5   Vector in 3d

P=(1, 7, 1) **Q=(7i+j+k)**
Q=(5, 3, 7) **P=(5i+3j+7k)**
QP=(5-1)i+(3-7)j+(7-1)k=4i-4j+6k
PQ=(4i-4j+6k)

Chanchal Dass, FIE, Email: cdass01@gmail.com, Mobile: +91-8320172787

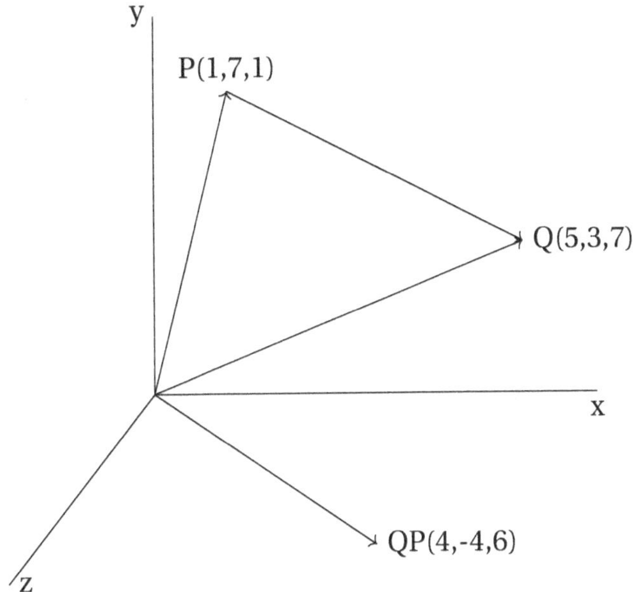

4.12.6 Vector Operations-Addition

Addition:**A+B**
A=(7i+2j+k) B=(5i+3j+k)
A+B=((7+5)i+(2+3)j+(1+1)k)=(12i+5j+2k)

Chanchal Dass, FIE, Email: cdass01@gmail.com, Mobile: +91-8320172787

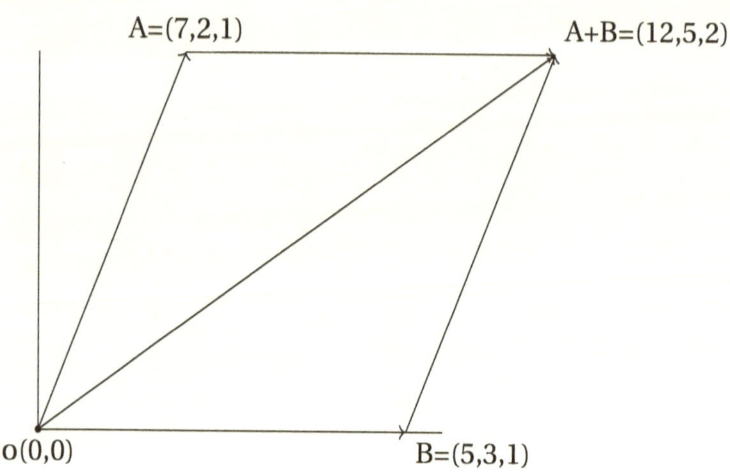

Figure 4.11: Vector Addition

4.12.7   Scalar Multiplication

C=(6i+4j+2k)
Multiplication of a vector by a scalar:
2*C=2*(6,4,2)=(12,8,4)

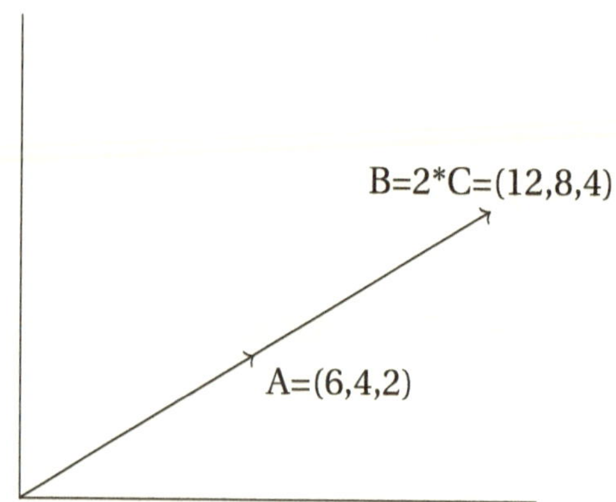

Figure 4.12: Scalar multiplication of vectors

The scalar multiplication of a vector makes it larger or smaller.

Chanchal Dass, FIE, Email: cdass01@gmail.com, Mobile: +91-8320172787

4.13   Vector Product

In vector algebra, there are two primary ways to multiply two vectors: the **dot product** (also known as the scalar product) and the **cross product** (also known as the vector product). Each of these operations combines two vectors to produce a result that is different in both type and interpretation. This is one of the issues that students face when learning vector product. My suggestion is that read the definitions carefully and draw the vectors as per definition. It will give you more clarity on vector products.

The vector product generally refers to these operations, with the dot product resulting in a scalar (a single number) and the cross product resulting in another vector.

4.13.1   Dot Product (Scalar Product)

The **dot product** of two vectors is an operation that takes two vectors and returns a single scalar quantity. This scalar represents the magnitude of one vector in the direction of another.

Definition

Given two vectors **A** and **B** in 2D or 3D space, the dot product is defined as:

$$\mathbf{A} \cdot \mathbf{B} = |\mathbf{A}||\mathbf{B}| \cos\theta$$

Where:

- $|\mathbf{A}|$ and $|\mathbf{B}|$ are the magnitudes of vectors **A** and **B**.

- θ is the angle between the two vectors.

Alternatively, in component form, if $\mathbf{A} = A_x\mathbf{i} + A_y\mathbf{j} + A_z\mathbf{k}$ and $\mathbf{B} = B_x\mathbf{i} + B_y\mathbf{j} + B_z\mathbf{k}$, then:

$$\mathbf{A} \cdot \mathbf{B} = A_x B_x + A_y B_y + A_z B_z$$

Properties of the Dot Product

- **Commutative Property:** $\mathbf{A} \cdot \mathbf{B} = \mathbf{B} \cdot \mathbf{A}$
- **Distributive Property:** $\mathbf{A} \cdot (\mathbf{B} + \mathbf{C}) = \mathbf{A} \cdot \mathbf{B} + \mathbf{A} \cdot \mathbf{C}$
- **Zero Vector:** $\mathbf{A} \cdot \mathbf{A} = |\mathbf{A}|^2$

4.13.2   Geometric Interpretation

The dot product measures how much one vector extends in the direction of another. Remember that it is not a vector. .

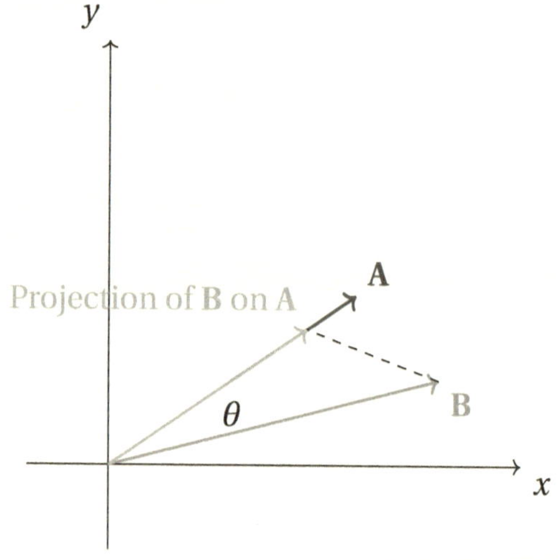

Figure 4.13: Projection of vector B on vector A

4.13.3   Example

If the vectors are perpendicular, the dot product is zero because $\cos 90° = 0$

Consider the vectors $\mathbf{A} = 2\mathbf{i} + 3\mathbf{j} + \mathbf{k}$ and $\mathbf{B} = \mathbf{i} - 2\mathbf{j} + 4\mathbf{k}$. The dot product is:

$$\mathbf{A} \cdot \mathbf{B} = 2 \times 1 + 3 \times (-2) + 1 \times 4 = 2 - 6 + 4 = 0$$

Since the dot product is zero, the vectors are perpendicular.

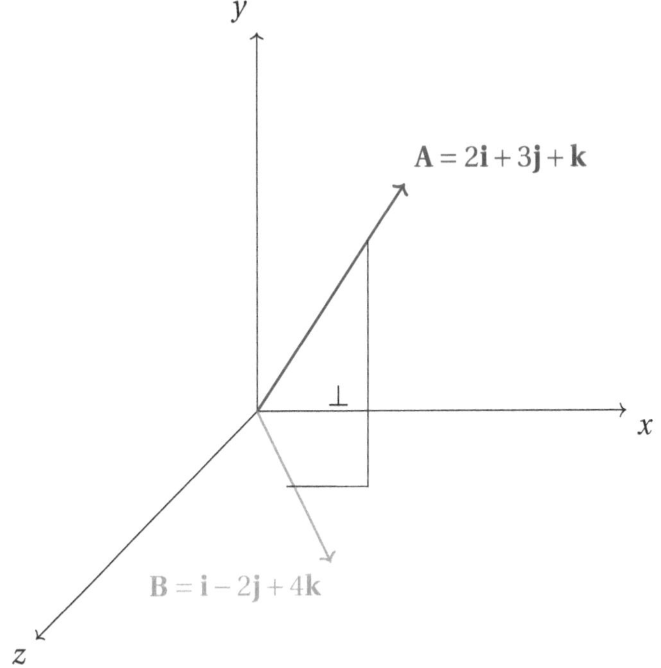

Figure 4.14: Vectors are at 90 degree if dot product is 0.

4.14 Cross Product (Vector Product)

"The **cross product**, also known as the **vector product**, is an operation that takes two vectors and returns a new vector that is perpendicular to the plane containing the original vectors. It's important to note that the cross product is specifically an operation in 3D space."

Explanation: The cross product indeed returns a vector perpendicular to the plane formed by the original two vectors. The cross product is defined only in three-dimensional space, as it relies on the concept of a plane formed by two vectors, which requires a third dimension for the resultant perpendicular vector.

4.14.1 Definition

Given two vectors **A** and **B** in 3D space, the cross product **C** is defined as:

$$C = A \times B$$

Where **C** is a vector whose magnitude is given by:

$$|C| = |A||B| \sin\theta$$

The direction of **C** is determined by the right-hand rule.

4.14.2 Graphical representation of Cross Product

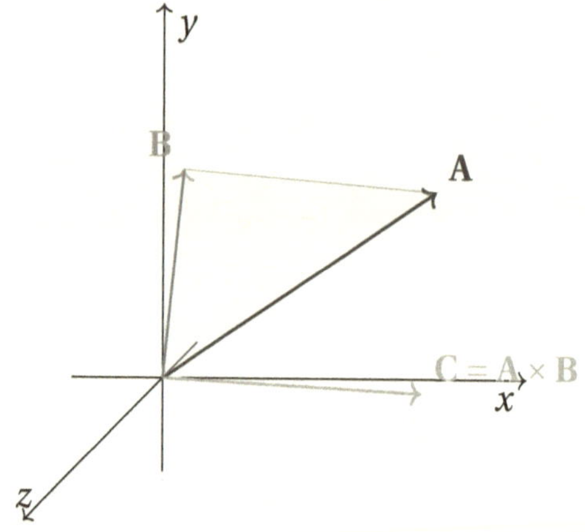

Figure 4.15: Geometry of Cross Product

Explanation:

1. Coordinate Axes: The x,y, and z axes are drawn to establish the 3D space.

2. The Vectors A and B: A is drawn in blue, B is drawn in red.

3. Cross Product Vector

   C: The cross product C=A×B is drawn in green, and it is perpendicular to the plane formed by A and B.

4. The Plane: A and B is shown in yellow with some transparency.

4.14.3 Mathematical Expression

If $\mathbf{A} = A_x\mathbf{i} + A_y\mathbf{j} + A_z\mathbf{k}$ and $\mathbf{B} = B_x\mathbf{i} + B_y\mathbf{j} + B_z\mathbf{k}$, then the cross product can be calculated by the determinant as given below:

$$\mathbf{C} = \begin{vmatrix} \mathbf{i} & \mathbf{j} & \mathbf{k} \\ A_x & A_y & A_z \\ B_x & B_y & B_z \end{vmatrix}$$

Expanding this determinant:

$$\mathbf{C} = (A_y B_z - A_z B_y)\mathbf{i} - (A_x B_z - A_z B_x)\mathbf{j} + (A_x B_y - A_y B_x)\mathbf{k}$$

Properties of the Cross Product

- **Anticommutative Property:** $\mathbf{A} \times \mathbf{B} = -(\mathbf{B} \times \mathbf{A})$
- **Distributive Property:** $\mathbf{A} \times (\mathbf{B} + \mathbf{C}) = \mathbf{A} \times \mathbf{B} + \mathbf{A} \times \mathbf{C}$
- **Zero Vector:** $\mathbf{A} \times \mathbf{A} = 0$

4.14.4 Geometric Interpretation

The magnitude of the cross product represents the area of the parallelogram formed by the two vectors. If the vectors are parallel, the cross product is zero because $\sin\theta = 0$.

Example

Consider the vectors $\mathbf{A} = 2\mathbf{i} + 3\mathbf{j} - \mathbf{k}$ and $\mathbf{B} = \mathbf{i} - 2\mathbf{j} + 4\mathbf{k}$. The cross product is:

$$\mathbf{C} = \begin{vmatrix} \mathbf{i} & \mathbf{j} & \mathbf{k} \\ 2 & 3 & -1 \\ 1 & -2 & 4 \end{vmatrix} = 10\mathbf{i} - 9\mathbf{j} - 7\mathbf{k}$$

Thus, $\mathbf{C} = 10\mathbf{i} - 9\mathbf{j} - 7\mathbf{k}$.

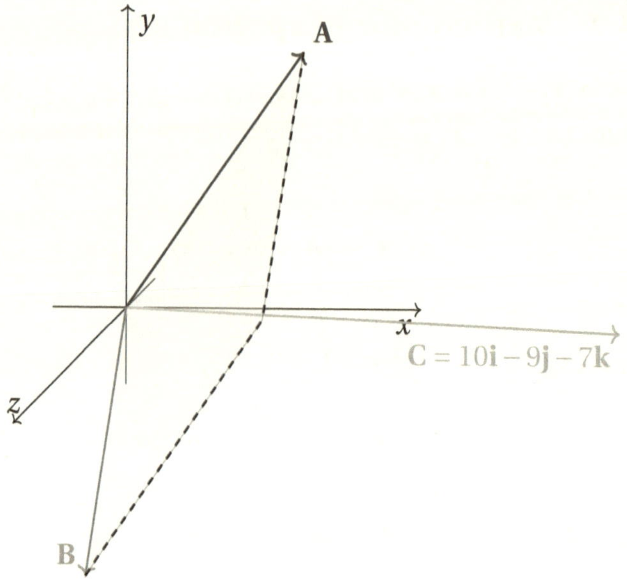

Figure 4.16: Cross Product

Explanation:

(a) Coordinate Axes: The x, y, and z axes are drawn to establish the 3D space.

(b) The Vectors A and B: $A = 2i + 3j - k$ is drawn in blue, $B = i - 2j + 4k$ is drawn in red.

(c) Cross Product Vector C: The cross product C=10i-9j-7k is drawn in green and is perpendicular to the plane formed by A and B.

(d) The Parallelogram: The parallelogram formed by the vectors A and B is shown with dashed lines and a shaded yellow area. The area of this parallelogram represents the magnitude of the cross product.

4.15 Comparison Between Dot Product and Cross Product

- The dot product yields a scalar, while the cross product yields a vector.
- The dot product measures the projection of one vector onto another, while the cross product measures the area of the parallelogram formed by the two vectors.
- The dot product is used in calculating angles and projections, while the cross product is used in finding perpendicular vectors and calculating torques.

4.15.1 Geometrical Interpretation of Dot Product

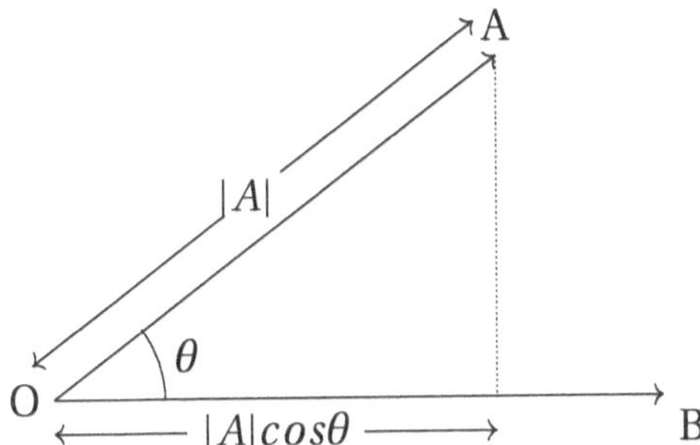

Figure 4.17: Dot product as projection

Projection of **A** on **B**

Maginitude of **projection of A on B**$=|A|cos\theta$

4.15.2 Projection of a vector on a vector

Magnitude of projection of a $= |a|cos\theta$
We know that a.b$=|a||b|cos\theta$
$\frac{a.b}{|b|}=|a|cos\theta$

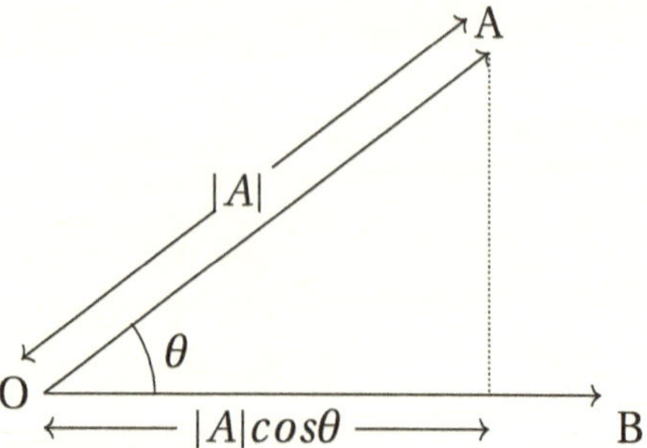

Figure 4.18: Projection of a vector

or Magnitude of Projection of a on b, $|a|cos\theta = \frac{(a.b)}{|b|}$
and unit vector in the direction of vector B=$\frac{b}{|b|}$

4.16 Finding Unit Vector

Let v=xi+yj+zk, Then $|v|=\sqrt{(x^2 + y^2 + z^2)}$
Unit Vector v = $\frac{(xi+yj+zk)}{\sqrt{(x^2+y^2+z^2)}}$
A unit vector is required for calculating the cross-product of Two
Vectors, finding projection vectors, etc. The projection vector of
a on b is p=$\frac{(a.b)}{|b|}\frac{b}{|b|}$

Basis: Unit vector in the direction of vector b and dot product of
it with vector a
Example:
Projection of vector A on vector B
A=4i+3j & B=5i

Here $|A|=\sqrt{(4^2 + 3^2)} = 5|B|= 5$
$A.B = (4i + 3j).(5i) = 4 * 5i.i + 3 * 5i.j = 20$
we can also find angle between two vectors from dot product
$A.B = |A||B|cos\theta$

Chanchal Dass, FIE, Email: cdass01@gmail.com, Mobile: +91-8320172787

$\implies 25\cos\theta=20 \implies \cos\theta=4/5=0.8$

we can also find angle between two vectors from dot product

Magnitude of projection of A on $B=|A|\cos\theta=5*0.8=4$

and the direction is $\frac{B}{|B|}=5i/5=i$

So projection of vector A on vector B=4i

4.16.1   Angle from Dot Product

Dot Product of two vectors A and B gives the angle formed by the vectors with MATLAB command

	Workspace
a=[2,5,4]	a = 2 5 4
b=[5,2,2]	b = 5 2 2
adotb=dot(a,b)	adotb = 28
absa=norm(a)	absa = 6.7082
absb=norm(b)	abs(b) = 5.7446
angle=acosd((adotb)/(absa*absb))	angle = 43.3980

4.16.2   Cross Product (Vector Product)

Definition:

$AxB=(AB\sin\theta)\, u_n$

where u_n is a unit vector The direction of vector u is perpendicular to the plane of vectors A and B.

Direction can be obtained by right-hand thumb rule with fingers rotation in the plane of vector A and B and from **A** toward **B** and thumb pointing in the direction of vector u.

Observations

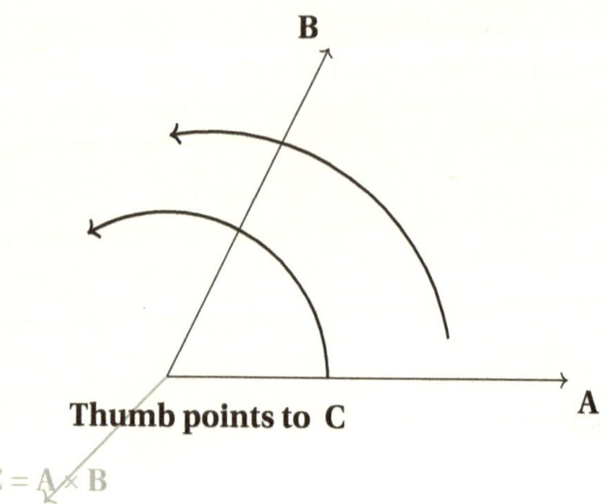

4.16.3   Computation of Cross Product

$$\mathbf{A} \times \mathbf{B} = \begin{bmatrix} i & j & k \\ A_x & A_y & A_z \\ B_x & B_y & B_z \end{bmatrix}$$

$$=(A_y * B_z - A_Z * B_y)\mathbf{i} + (A_z * B_x - A_x * B_z)\mathbf{j} + (A_x * B_y - B_x * A_y)\mathbf{k}$$

Example:

A=(2, -2, 1), B=(3, 4, 12)

$$\mathbf{AXB} = \begin{bmatrix} i & j & k \\ 2 & -2 & 1 \\ 3 & 4 & 12 \end{bmatrix}$$

$$= [(-2 * 12 - 4 * 1)\mathbf{i} + (1 * 3 - 2 * 12)\mathbf{j} + (2 * 4 - 3 * -2)\mathbf{k}]$$

$$- 28\mathbf{i} - 21\mathbf{j} + 1\mathbf{k}$$

$$A \times B = [-28, -21, 14]$$

5. AxB=$|A||B|sin(t)$**n** (n=unit vector along normal)

Observations:

1. axb is a vector

2. axb is 0 iff the two vectors are parallel or collinear

3. If t=90 then AxB=$|A||B|$**n**

Chanchal Dass, FIE, Email: cdass01@gmail.com, Mobile: +91-8320172787

4. **ixi=jxj=kxk=0** and **ixj=k, jxk=i, kxi=j**

5. $\sin(t)=|\mathbf{A} \times \mathbf{B}|/|A||B|$

6. ixj#jxi(NON-COMMUTATIVE)

4.16.4   How Vector Product Finds Area?

Vector product axb is only defined when
a=(a_1,a_2,a_3) and b = (b_1,b_2,b_3)
have three elements or three dimension vectors

$$a \times b = (a_2 b_3 - a_3 b_2,\ a_3 b_1 - a_1 b_3,\ a_1 b_2 - a_2 b_1)$$
$$|a \times b|^2 = (a_2 b_3 - a_3 b_2)^2 + (a_3 b_1 - a_1 b_3)^2 + (a_1 b_2 - a_2 b_1)^2$$
$$|a \times b|^2 = a_2{}^2 b_3{}^2 + a_3{}^2 b_2{}^2 - 2a_2\, a_3\, b_2\, b_3 + a_3{}^2 b_1{}^2 + a_1{}^2 b_3{}^2 - 2a_1\, a_3\, b_1\, b_3 + a_1{}^2 b_2{}^2 + a_2{}^2 b_1{}^2 - 2a_1\, a_2\, b_1\, b_2$$

$$|a \times b|^2 = (a_1{}^2 + a_2{}^2 + a_3{}^2)(b_1{}^2 + b_2{}^2 + b_3{}^2) - (a_1\, b_1 + a_2\, b_2 + a_3\, b_3)^2$$
$$|a \times b|^2 = |a|^2||b|^2 - (a.b)^2$$
$$|a \times b|^2 = |a|^2||b|^2 - |a|^2|b|^2 \cos(t)^2$$
$$|a \times b|^2 = |a|^2||b|^2 (1 - \cos(t)^2)$$
$$|a \times b|^2 = |a|^2||b|^2 \sin(t)^2)$$
$$|a \times b| = |a||b|\sin(t)$$

$a \times b$ is a vector perpendicular to a and b
and its length is $|a \times b| = |a||b|\sin(t)$

4.16.5   Finding Area of a Triangle

AxB=$|A||B|\sin(t)\mathbf{n}$ (n=unit vector along normal)
Area of the triangle formed by the vectors as adjacent sides is

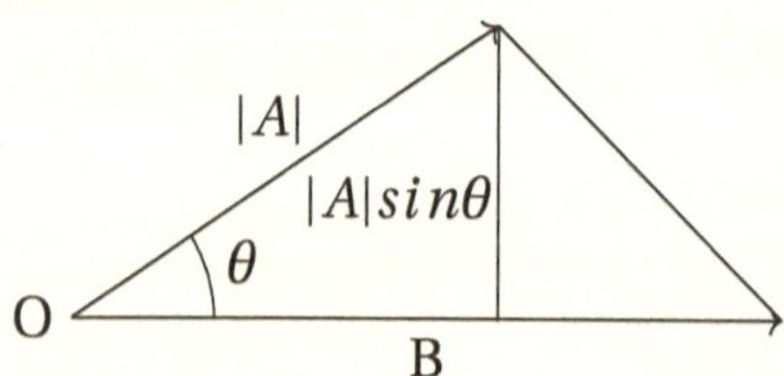

Area=1/2 base x Height

$$=1/2 * |A||B|\sin(t)$$

Area of the parallelogram formed by the vectors as adjacent sides is

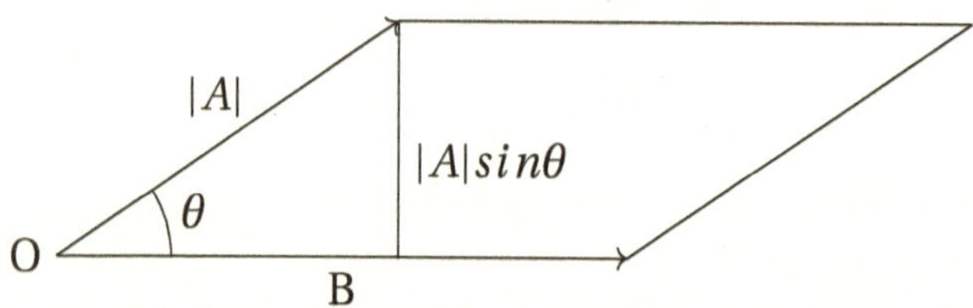

Area= base x Height

$$=|A| |B|\sin(t)$$

visualisation of Cross Product

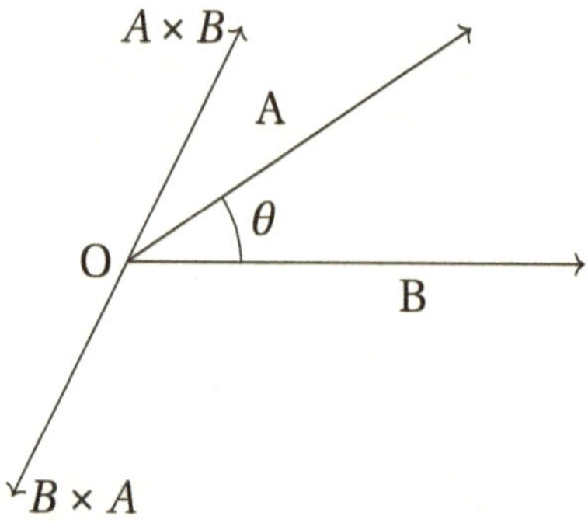

4.16.6   Scalar Triple Product

A=(7,2,1),**B**=(5,3,1),**C**=(6,4,2)
Scalar triple product **(AxB).C**
=(7i+2j+k)X(5i+3j+k).(6i+4j+2k)
==(-i-2j+11k).(6i+4j+2k)=8

4.17   Volume of parallelopiped formed by the three vectors

The Parallelepiped formed by three vectors A,B & C is

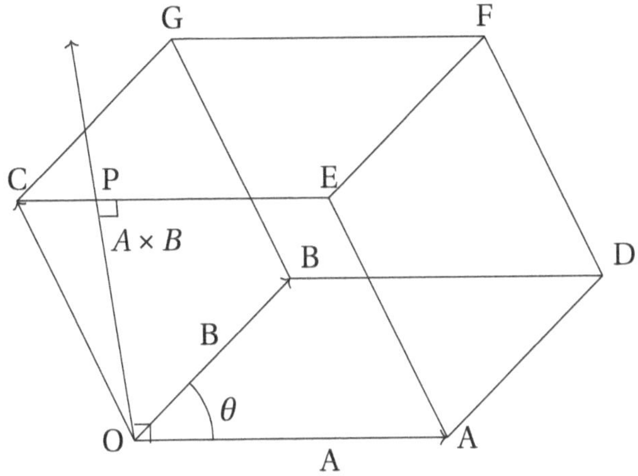

The Volume of parallelepiped(OADBCEFG)
=Perpendicular distance between two parallel faces
x Area of any of the two parallel faces

= ×Area of parallelogram $OADB$ $(\mathrm{ar}(OADB) = |\vec{A} \times \vec{B}|)$
Now OP=Perpendcular distance between two surfaces OABD and
CEFG
As **AXB** direction is perpendicular to two surfaces taking projection of

C on AXB gives OP

So, OP=$(AXB).C/\ |A \times B|$

So, $OP \times |A \times B| = (A \times B).C$

So, Area of paralellepiped formed by three vectors **A**,**B** and **C** is **A**$\times$**B.C**

Example:

A=(7,2,1),**B**=(5,3,1),**C**=(6,4,2)

volume of paralellepiped formed by **A**,**B**,**C** =

Scalar triple product **(AxB).C**

=(7i+2j+k)X(5i+3j+k).(6i+4j+2k)

==(-i-2j+11k).(6i+4j+2k)=8

Scalar triple product using matrix

A=(7,2,1),**B**=(5,3,1),**C**=(6,4,2)

Scalar triple product **(AxB).C**

=Det of matrix $\begin{bmatrix} 6 & 4 & 2 \\ 7 & 2 & 1 \\ 5 & 3 & 1 \end{bmatrix}$

=8

4.18   Torque

Stewart Page 758: Ex-6:

Force=40N at 75°

Distance= 0.25 m

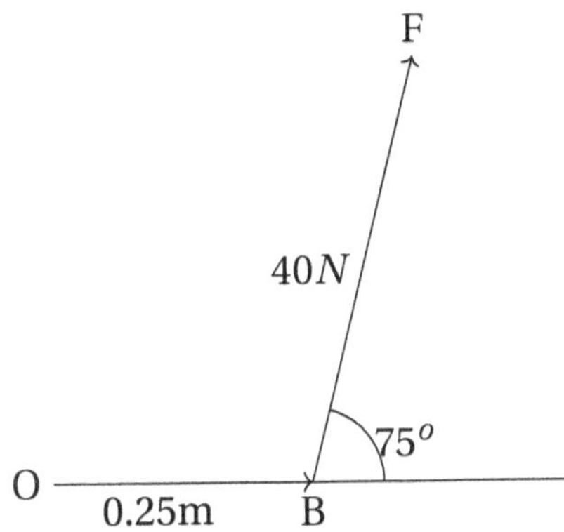

Here, the magnitude of force and distance are given.

t=$r \times f$

Magnitude of torque = $|t|=|r|\,|f|$ sin(t)

$|t|=40 * .25 * sin(75^o)$=9.66 N.m

The torque is 9.66 N.m.

Chapter 5

Three Dimensional Geometry and Vectors

In dealing with 3-dimensional geometry with Cartesian coordinate system, many times, it becomes difficult to analyze different concepts related to it. The use of Vectors makes the study of three-dimensional problems very simple and effective. Topics covered:

1. Direction cosines and direction ratios of a line
2. Direction cosines and direction ratios of a line joining two points
3. Equation of lines
4. Equation of Planes
5. Distance between lines
6. Distance between a point and a plane

5.0.1 Direction Ratios

- Direction ratios provide a convenient way of specifying the direction of a line in three-dimensional space.
- Direction cosines are the cosines of the angles between a line and the coordinate axes.
- Given a vector $r = ai + bj + ck$, its direction ratios are $a : b : c$.
- This means that to move in the direction of the vector we must move a units in the x direction and b units in the y direction for every c units in the z-direction.

5.0.2   Direction cosines as l m n

- If a directed line passing through origin and makes angle α , β,γ with x, y, z axis then these angles are called direction angles and cosine of these angles $\cos(\alpha)$, $\cos(\beta)$ and $\cos(\gamma)$ are called direction cosines.

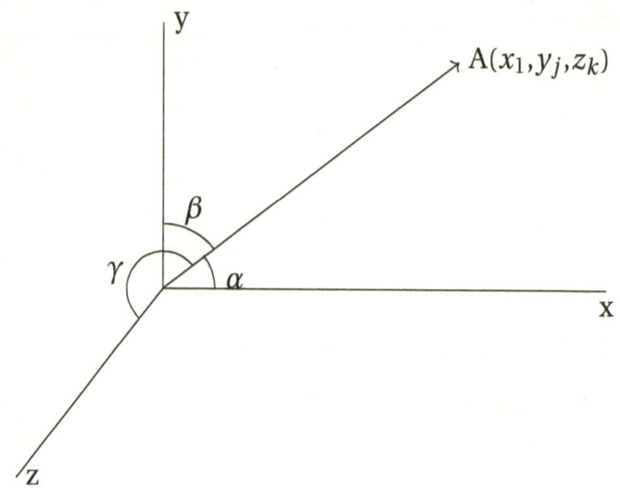

- If we reverse the direction of the line, then the direction cosines will be $\cos(\pi + \alpha)$, $\cos(\pi + \beta)$ and $\cos(\pi + \gamma)$ and $-\cos(\alpha)$,$-\cos(\beta)$ and $-\cos(\gamma)$.

- As same line should not have two direction ratios, we take l, m, n as direction cosines.

5.0.3   Direction Cosines

a=[2,3,1]

$|a|$=3.741

l=cosα=2/3.741

m=cosβ=3/3.741

n=cosγ=1/3.741

Direction cosines of a line passing through 2 point

A=[2,3,1] B=[3,5,2]

AB=(3-2)i+(5-3)j+(2-1)k=i+2j+k

$|AB|$ =2.45

l=cosα=1/2.45=0.41

m=cosβ=2/2.45=0.82

n=cosγ=1/2.45=0.41

5.0.4 Direction Ratios

a=[2,3,5] r=$|a|$=6.1644

l=cosα=2/6.1644

m=cosβ=3/6.1644

n=cosγ=5/6.1644

dir_cosines=0.3244 0.4867 0.8111

angles= 1.2404 1.0625 0.6248

angles_degree =71.0682 60.8784 35.7598

Direction Angles=α,β,γ

Direction Cosines=l, m, n = x/$|a|$, y/$|a|$, z/$|a|$ l=x/r, m=y/r, n=z/r

Direction Ratios=x, y, z=2, 3, 5

x=l r, y=m r, z= n r

5.0.5 Equation of a line in space (Vector representation of line)

- A line in 3d is uniquely determined if
    1. it passes through given point and has given direction
    2. It passes through given points

5.0.6 Vector Equation of Line Passing Through a point and parallel to a vector b

Point P=[5,2,-4]

Vector **v**=[3,2-8]

a(P)	-1	7	1
b(V)	5	3	7
o	0	0	0
2b(λ=2)	10	6	14
r=a+λ b(λ=2)	9	13	15

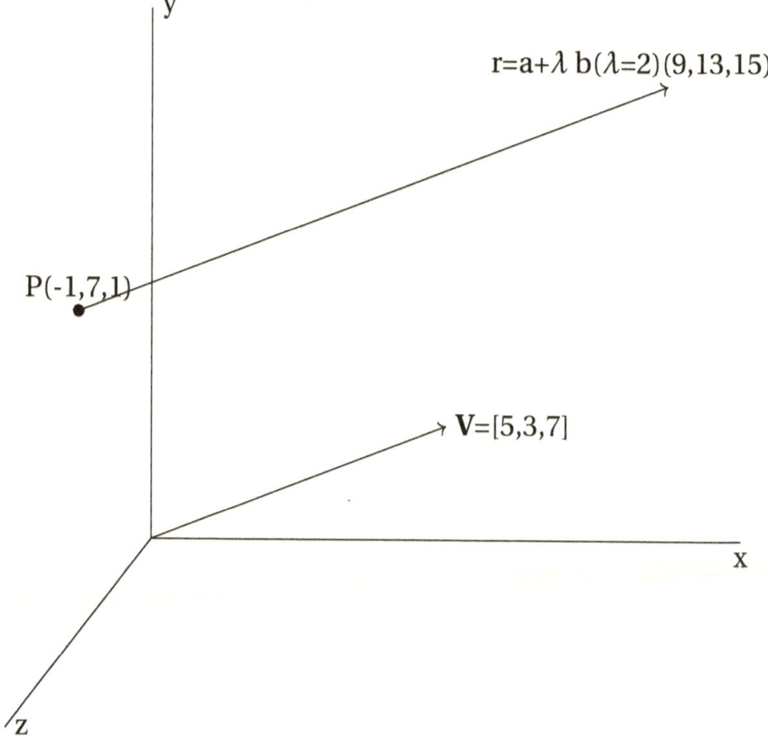

We are required to find a vector r which will represent a line
From Triangular law of vector addition,

λ b=r-a or r=a+λ b, λ is a parameter and can assume any arbitrary
value.

Equation of Line derivation of Cartesian form from vector form Let

the coordinate of given point A is $(x_0 + y_0 + z_0)$
And Direction ratios of the line l are a, b, c
Then, $a = x_0 i + y_0 j + z_0 k$ $b = ai + bj + zk$
We have to find out, $r = xi + yj + zk = (x_0 + \lambda a)i + (y_0 + \lambda b)j + (z_0 + \lambda c)k$
We know $r = a + \lambda b$, λ is a parameter and can assume any arbitrary value.
Hence, $x = x_0 + \lambda a$ $y = y_0 + \lambda b$ $z = z_0 + \lambda c$
From these equations, we can write, $(x - x_0)/a = (y - y_0)/b = (z - z_0)/c = \lambda$

Example of the vector and Cartesian equation

Find the vector and Cartesian equation of the line through the point a=(5, 2, -4) and which is parallel to the vector b=3i+2j-8k.
Vector equation is $r = a + \lambda\, b$
Hence, $r = 5i + 2j - 4k + \lambda * (3i + 2j - 8k)$
For Cartesian equation, $r = xi + yj + zk = (5 + 3\lambda)i + (2 + 2\lambda)j + (-4 - 8)k$
$(x-5)/3 = (y-2)/2 = (z+4)/-8 = t$
Parametric Equation: x=3t+5, y=2+2t. z=-4+8t
Vector equation is $r = a + \lambda b$
Hence, $r = 5i + 2j - 4k + \lambda * (3i + 2j - 8k)$
For Cartesian equation, $r = xi + yj + zk = (5 + 3\lambda)i + (2 + 2\lambda)j + (-4 - 8)k$
$(x-5)/3 = (y-2)/2 = (z+4)/-8$

5.0.7   Vector Equation of Line Passing Through Two points

A line passing through two given points P=[-1,7,1] and Q=[4,10,8]:

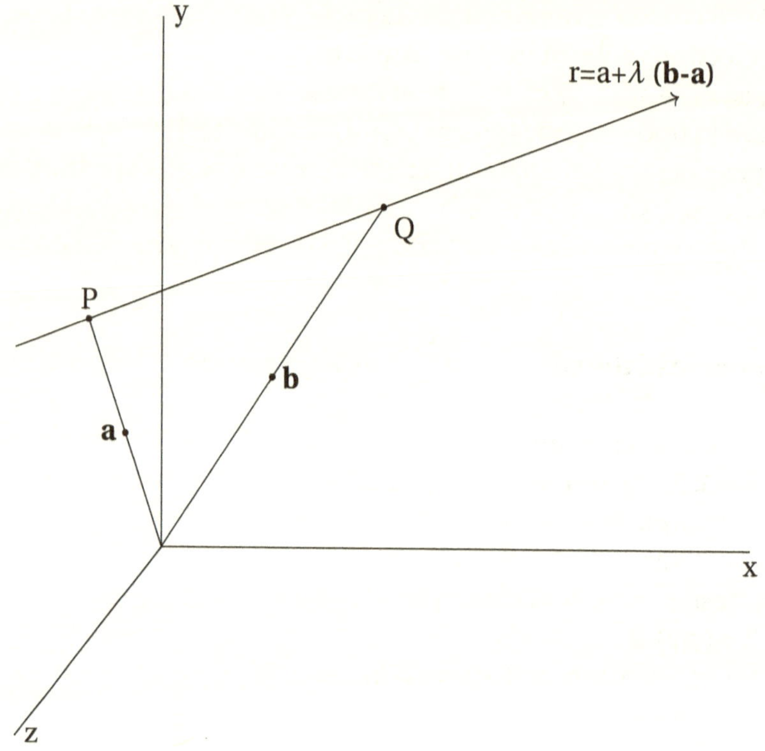

Line passing through point PQ will be parallel to vector PQ
Vector PQ is **b-a**
So now we can find equation of line using Previous method where a
point(P) and parallel vector(b-a) is given
r=a+λ (b-a) where λ is a parameter and can assume any arbitrary value

Equation of Line derivation of Cartesian form from vector form
Let the coordinate of given points are $a = x_1 + y_1 + z_1$ $b = x_2 + y_2 + z_2$
We know r=a+λ(b-a), λ is a parameter and can assume any arbitrary
value.
We have to find out, r=xi+yj+zk= a+λ (b-a)
$=(x_1+\lambda (x_2 - x_1))i + (y_1+\lambda(y_2 - y_1)j + (z_1+\lambda(z_2 - z_1))k$
Hence, $x = x_1+\lambda(x_2 - x_1)$
$y=y_1+\lambda(y_2 - y_1)$ and $z = z_1+\lambda(z_2 - z_1)$

From this equations, we can write
$$(x - x_1)/(x_2 - x_1) = (y - y_1)/(x_2 - x_1) = (z - z_1)/(x_2 - x_1)$$

5.0.8   Angle Between two Lines

Case-1

When lines pass from origin

Let $l_1 = [a_1, b_1, c_1]$ and $l_2 = [a_2, b_2, c_2]$ direction ratios

We know that the directed lines are vectors with components as a, b, c (a, b, c are direction ratios)

Now from dot product we can write, $cos(t) = a.b/|a||b|$

Or

$$cos(t) = |a_1 a_2 + b_1 b_2 + c_1 c_2/((\sqrt{(a_1^2 + b1^2 + c_1^2)} * \sqrt{(a_2^2 + b_2^2 + c_2^2)})|$$

Case-2

When lines do not pass from origin

Let $l_1 = [a_1, b_1, c_1] l_2 = [a_2, b_2, c_2]$ direction ratios

Here we will take two line pass through origin and parallel to given line.

We know that the directed lines are vectors with components as a, b, c (a, b, c are direction ratios)

Now from dot product we can write, cos(t)=a.b/|a||b|

Or

$$cos(t) = |(a_1 a_2 + b_1 b_2 + c_1 c_2)/((\sqrt{(a_1^2 + b_1^2 + c_1^2)} * \sqrt{(a_2^2 + b_2^2 + c_2^2)})|$$

Case-3 When the direction cosines are given

Let $l_1 = [l_1, m_1, n_1]$ and $l_2 = [l_2, m_2, n_2]$ direction ratios

Here we will take two line pass through origin and parallel to given line.

We know that the directed lines are vectors with components as l,m,n

Now from dot product we can write, cos(t)=a.b/|a||b|

Or

$$cos(t)=|(l_1 l_2 + m_1 m_2 + n_1 n_2)/((\sqrt{(l_1^2 + m_1^2 + n_1^2)} * \sqrt{(l_2^2 + m_2^2 + n_2^2)})|$$

Case-4 When the angle is 90^0, $|l_1 l_2 + m_1 m_2 + n_1 n_2|=0$

Case-5 When the angle is 0 degree, the $a_1/a_2 = b_1/b_2 = c_1/c_2$

5.0.9   Shortest Distance Between Two Lines

Case-1 When two lines intersect, then shortest distance is 0

Shortest distance=0;

Case-2

When two lines are parallel- Then the distance between them is the perpendicular distance. This the length of the perpendicular drawn from a point in one line on the other line.

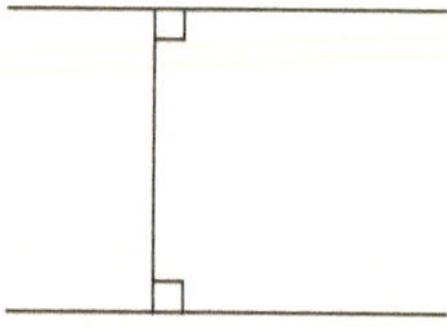

Shortest distance= Perpendicular Distance

Case-3 In space or 3d, there may be lines that are neither intersect nor parallel. These lines are non coplanar and called skew lines.
For skew lines, the line of shortest distance is the line perpendicular to both the lines

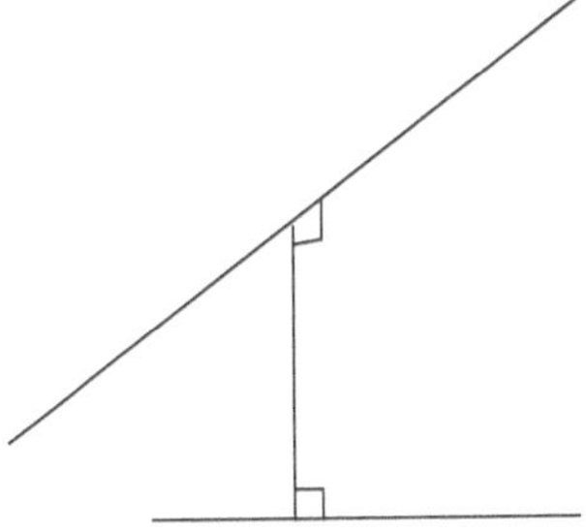

Shortest distance= Perpendicular Distance

5.0.10 Shortest Distance Between Two Skew Lines

We know that the cross product gives us the perpendicular to both vectors

Let, $l_1 = a_1 + \lambda b_1$ and $l_2 = a_2 + \mu b_2$, Hence a_1 and a_2 are two points on lines l_1 and l_2. Let these points are S and T.

Then the magnitude of the shortest distance vector will be equal to the projection of ST along the line of shortest distance.

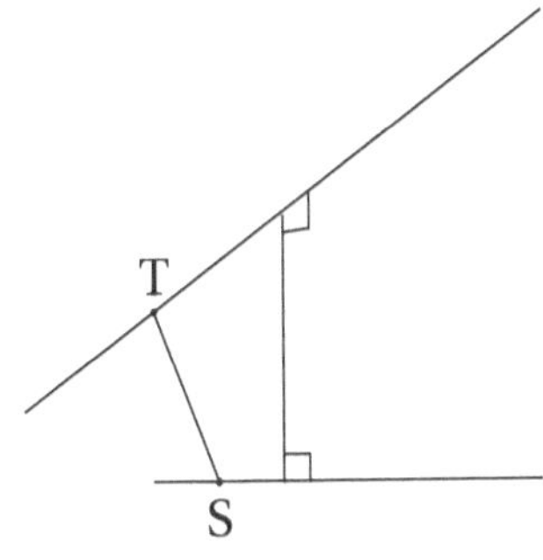

Shortest distance=Perpendicular Distance

For calculating the shortest, follow the following step

Given vectors are $l_1 = a_1 + \lambda b_1$ and $l_2 = a_2 + \mu b_2$

1. Calculate the perpendicular Vector to b_1 and $b_2 = b_1 \times b_2$

Chanchal Dass, FIE, Email: cdass01@gmail.com, Mobile: +91-8320172787

2. Step-2: Calculate unit vector along $b_1 \times b_2 = \frac{b_1 \times b_2}{|b_1 \times b_2|}$

3. Calculate ST=a_2-a_1

4. Calculate d= ST cos(t)

5. Calculate $\cos(t) = |\frac{PQ.ST}{|PQ||ST|}|$

6. Calculate $d = |ST|\cos(t) = |ST||\frac{PQ.ST}{|PQ||ST|}|$

   or d=$|\frac{PQ.ST}{|PQ|}|=|\frac{b_1 \times b_2.(a_2-a_1)}{|b_1 \times b_2|}|$

When the lines are in Cartesian form:

Then $l_1 = x - x_1/a_1 = y - y_1/b_1 = z - z_1/c_1$

And $l_2 = x - x_2/a_2 = y - y_2/a_2 = z - z_2/c_2$

Shortest distance=Perpendicular Distance

$$\text{mat(A)}=\begin{bmatrix} 6 & 4 & 2 \\ 7 & 2 & 1 \\ 5 & 3 & 1 \end{bmatrix} \quad \text{Then, } d=\frac{det(A)}{|\sqrt{(b_1 c_2 - c_2 a_1)^2 + (c_1 a_2 - c_2 a_1)^2 + (a_1 b_2 - b_1 a_2)^2}|}$$

5.0.11   Shortest Distance Between Parallel Lines

We know that the cross product gives us the perpendicular to both vectors

Let, $l_1 = a_1 + \lambda b$ and $l_2 = a_2 + \mu b$,

Hence a_1 and a_2 are two points on lines l_1 and l_2. Let these points are S and T.

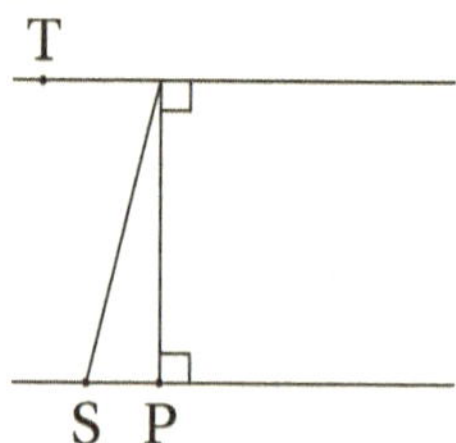

   Shortest distance= Perpendicular Distance

   As the lines are parallel then b is same for both the line

Then the magnitude of the shortest distance vector will be equal to the projection of ST along the line of shortest distance TP.

Let t be the angle between the vectors ST and b, then bxST=$|b||ST|sin(t)n$

Now ST=a2-a1

$$bx(a2 - a1) = |b|PT * 1$$

Hence, d=TP=$\frac{|b\times(a2-a1)|}{|b|}$

5.0.12 Plane

A plane is determined uniquely if any one of the following parameters is known:

1. The normal of the plane and its distance from the origin. It is the equation of plane in normal form.

2. It passes through a point and perpendicular of a given direction

3. It passes through three given non collinear points

5.0.13 Equation of a plane in normal form

The normal of the plane and its distance from the origin is given. We have to find the equation of plane in normal form.

Let the normal vector , **v**=a**i**+b**j**+ c**k**

Perpendicular Distance of the plane from the origin is d

First calculate unit normal vector, **n**= $\frac{\mathbf{v}}{|\mathbf{v}|}$

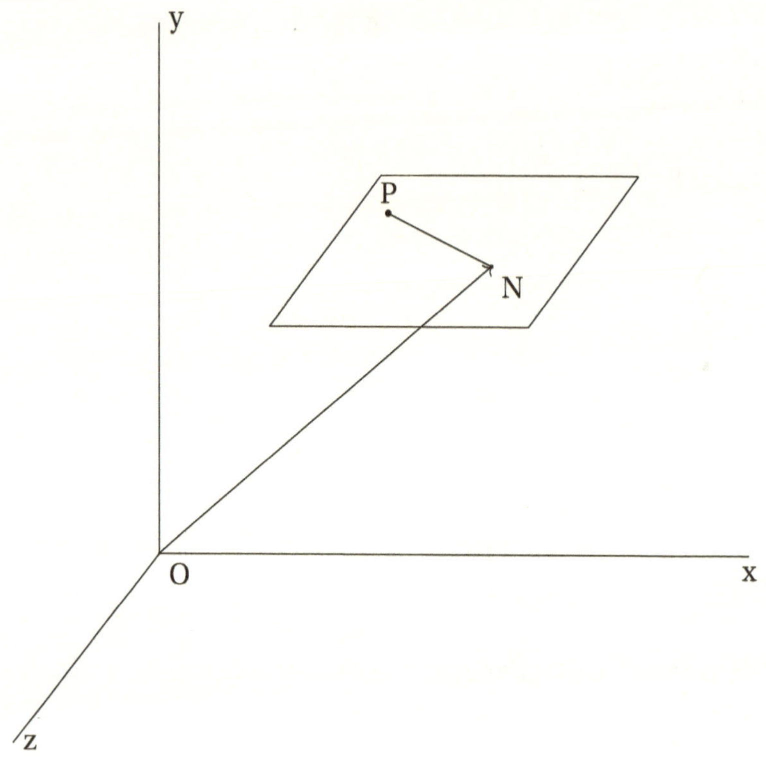

Consider a plane whose perpendicular distance (ON) from the origin is d and **n** is unit normal vector. Then ON = **dn**

Let **r** be the position vector of the point P and P(x, y, z) be any point in the plane. Hence NP is perpendicular to ON.

Hence dot product of ON and PN is 0, i.e., ON.PN=0 $1cm$ (i)

Now, OP=ON+NP (Triangular Law of Vector Addition)

Or **r=dn+NP**

Or NP=**r-dn**   (ii)

Now, from (i), **dr.(r-dn)=0**, Or **n.(r-dn)=0**(As d#0) Or **nr-dnn=0**

Or **n.r=d** as (**n.n=1**)

This is the vector form of the plane

where **n** is the unit normal vector **r** is position vector OP or **r=xi+yj+zk**

The Cartesian form is **nx*x+ny*y+nz*z=d**

Drawing a plane in normal form

Chanchal Dass, FIE, Email: cdass01@gmail.com, Mobile: +91-8320172787

Given: The normal of the plane and its distance from the origin.

r.n=d

This is the vector form of the plane

To draw the plane, we require to convert it to Cartesian form:

nx*x+**n**y*y+**n**z*z=d

5.0.14 Drawing a plane in normal form

Given normal is [2 − 34] and the perpendicular distance=$\frac{6}{\sqrt{29}}$

Unit normal-[$\frac{2}{\sqrt{29}}$**i**-$\frac{3}{\sqrt{29}}$**j**+$\frac{4}{\sqrt{29}}$

r.n=d

[x**i**+y**j**+z**k**].[0.371390676**i**- 0.557086015**j**+0.742781353**k**]=1.114172029

Or 0.371390676xi-0.557086015yj+ 0.742781353zk]=1.114172029

For Plotting in MATLAB:

xx=-5:.1:5

yy=xx

[x,y]=meshgrid(xx,yy)

z=(1.114172029-0.371390676*x+0.557086015*y)/0.742781353

surf(x,y,z)

hold on

plot3([0 2],[0 -3],[0 4],'oy-')

plot3([0 0.371390676],[0 -0.557086015],[0 0.742781353],'or')

The normal of the plane and its distance from the origin is given. It is required to find the equation of the plane in normal form.

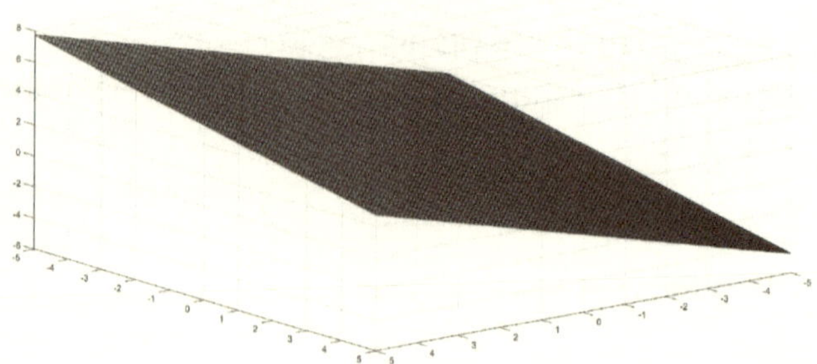

5.0.15 Equation of a plane perpendicular to a given vector and passing through a given point

There can be many planes that are perpendicular to the given vector.
Through a given point P(x0, y0, z0), only one such plane exists.
Let a plane pass through a point A with position vector a perpendicular to the vector N.
Let r be the position vector of any point P(x, y, z) in the plane.
Then the point P lies in the plane if and only if AP is perpendicular to N, i.e., AP.N=0.
But AP=r-a.
Therefore, (r-a).N=0
Cartesian Form:
Given Point A be (x0, y0, z0)
Direction ratios of N=Ai+Bj+Ck
r=xi+yj+zk
(r-a).N=0
So [(x-x0)i+(y-y0)j+(z-z0)k].[Ai+Bj+Ck]=0
A(x-xo)+B(y-y0)+C(z-z0)=0

Example

Find the vector and Cartesian equation of the plane passing through the point (5, 2, -4) and perpendicular to the line with direction ratios 2,3, -1.

Chanchal Dass, FIE, Email: cdass01@gmail.com, Mobile: +91-8320172787

Point is (5,2,-4), hence Position vector is P=5i+2j-4k
Normal vector N=2i+3j-k
Let the Vector representing the plane R=xi+yj+zk
From dot product, we get, (R-P).N=0
Cartesian form:
(x-5)*2+(y-2)*3+(z+4)*-1=0
2x+3y-z=20
z=(20-2x-3y)/-1
2x+3y-z=20
xx=-5:.1:5;
yy=xx; [x,y]=meshgrid(xx,yy);
z=(-20+2*x+3*y);
surf(x,y,z)
hold on
plot3([0 2],[0 3],[0 -1],'^m-')
There can be many plane to a perpendicular line
xx=-5:.1:5;
yy=xx;
[x,y]=meshgrid(xx,yy);
z=(-20+2*x+3*y);
surf(x,y,z)
hold on
plot3([0 2],[0 3],[0 -1],'^m-')
z1=(10-2*x-3*y)/-1;
z2=(30-2*x-3*y)/-1;
surf(x,y,z1)
surf(x,y,z2)

5.0.16 Equation of a Plane Passing Through Three Non-Collinear Points

To find the equation of a plane passing through three non-collinear points $A(x_1, y_1, z_1)$, $B(x_2, y_2, z_2)$, and $C(x_3, y_3, z_3)$, we use the vector form of the equation of a plane:

$$\mathbf{r} \cdot (\mathbf{AB} \times \mathbf{AC}) = \mathbf{OA} \cdot (\mathbf{AB} \times \mathbf{AC})$$

Where:

- $\mathbf{r}$ is the position vector (x, y, z),
- $\mathbf{AB}$ and $\mathbf{AC}$ are vectors between the points,
- $\times$ represents the cross product.

The scalar form of the plane equation can be written as:

$$a(x - x_1) + b(y - y_1) + c(z - z_1) = 0$$

Where (a, b, c) is the normal vector to the plane, obtained from the cross product **AB** × **AC**.

Example: Consider points $A(1, 2, 3)$, $B(4, 0, -1)$, and $C(0, 1, 2)$.

- Compute **AB** and **AC**.
- Find the cross product **AB** × **AC** to get the normal vector.
- Use the normal vector in the plane equation.

5.0.17 Why is it Necessary That the Three Points Should be Non-Collinear?

If three points are collinear, they lie on a single straight line, and an infinite number of planes can pass through this line. Therefore, specifying a unique plane requires the points to be non-collinear.

Example: Consider three collinear points lying along the spine of a book. Many planes can pass through the book's spine, representing different orientations of the book in space. However, if the three points are not collinear, like the corners of the book cover, only one plane can pass through these three points, representing the plane of the book cover.

5.0.18 Intercept Form of the Equation of a Plane

The intercept form of the equation of a plane is given by:

$$\frac{x}{a} + \frac{y}{b} + \frac{z}{c} = 1$$

Where:

- a, b, and c are the intercepts on the x-, y-, and z-axes, respectively.

Example: For a plane cutting the x-axis at $a = 4$, the y-axis at $b = 3$, and the z-axis at $c = 6$, the equation is:

$$\frac{x}{4} + \frac{y}{3} + \frac{z}{6} = 1$$

5.0.19 Coplanarity of Two Lines

Two lines are coplanar if they lie on the same plane. The condition for two lines $\mathbf{r_1} = \mathbf{a_1} + \lambda\mathbf{b_1}$ and $\mathbf{r_2} = \mathbf{a_2} + \mu\mathbf{b_2}$ to be coplanar is:

$$(\mathbf{a_2} - \mathbf{a_1}) \cdot (\mathbf{b_1} \times \mathbf{b_2}) = 0$$

Example: For lines, $\mathbf{r_1} = (1,2,3) + \lambda(1,-1,2)$ and $\mathbf{r_2} = (2,1,4) + \mu(2,-2,1)$, check if the lines satisfy the coplanarity condition.

5.0.20 Angle Between Two Planes

The angle θ between two planes with normal vectors $\mathbf{n_1}$ and $\mathbf{n_2}$ is given by:

$$\cos\theta = \frac{\mathbf{n_1} \cdot \mathbf{n_2}}{|\mathbf{n_1}||\mathbf{n_2}|}$$

Example: For planes $x + 2y + 2z = 3$ and $2x + y + 2z = 5$, find the angle between them by calculating the dot product of their normal vectors.

5.0.21 Distance of a Point from a Plane

The perpendicular distance d from a point $P(x_1, y_1, z_1)$ to a plane $ax + by + cz + d = 0$ is given by:

$$d = \frac{|ax_1 + by_1 + cz_1 + d|}{\sqrt{a^2 + b^2 + c^2}}$$

Example: For a plane $3x + 4y - z + 10 = 0$ and point $P(1,2,3)$, calculate the distance using the above formula.

5.0.22 Angle Between a Line and a Plane

The angle θ between a line with direction vector $\mathbf{b}$ and a plane with normal vector $\mathbf{n}$ is given by:

$$\sin\theta = \frac{\mathbf{b}\cdot\mathbf{n}}{|\mathbf{b}||\mathbf{n}|}$$

Example: For a line $\mathbf{r} = (2,-1,3) + \lambda(1,2,2)$ and plane $2x - y + 2z = 5$, find the angle between them by computing the dot product of the direction and normal vectors.

Appendix 1

The following presentation provides a simple, practical, and precise overview of the entire subject of vector algebra. Readers can use this presentation for modeling in MS Excel and check the validity of each concept

Vector Algebra

What is Vector?

19-02-2022

Vector Algebra

2

Why the study of vector is at is Vector?

19-02-2022

Vector Algebra

- Locating a point in 2d as well as 3d.
- Distance between two point,
- Unit lengths
- Equation of lines and planes
- Angle between two lines
- Areas of a triangle
- Normal to a plane
- Section formulas
- Projection of a line

19-02-2022

Vector Algebra

(4)

What is Vector?

A vector is the quantity that has magnitude and direction.

Directed Line Segment-A directed Line segment has magnitude and Direction. Hence, geometrically, any vector can be represented as a directed line

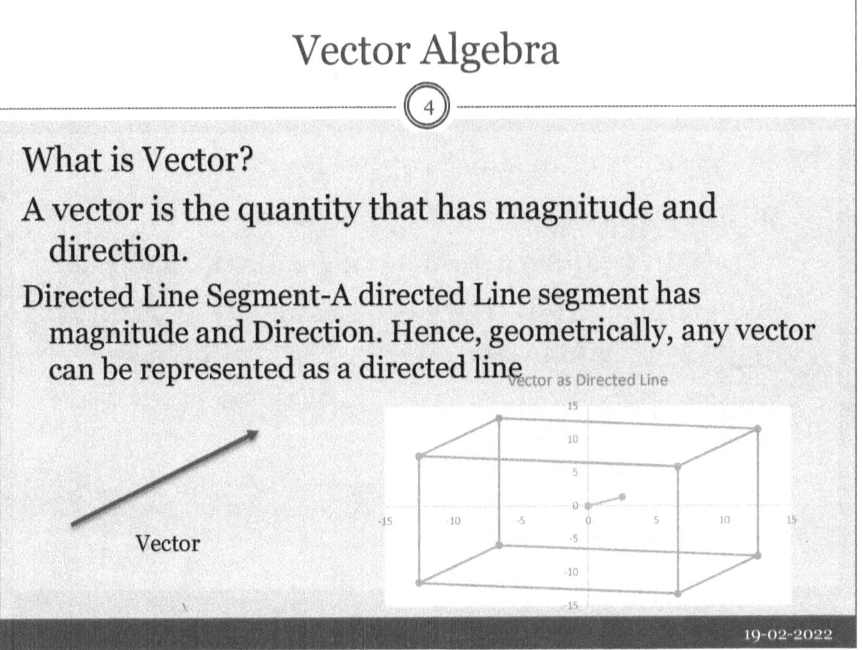

Type of vectors

- Zero Vector-initial and terminal point coincide
- Unit vector-A vector whose magnitude is unity,
- Co-initial Vectors-Vectors having same initial point
- Collinear Vectors-If they are parallel to the same line
- Equal Vectors-Same magnitude and Direction
- Negative Vector- Same magnitude but opposite direction

19-02-2022

Addition of Vectors

(6)

Triangle law of vector addition:

For Vector Addition, Place initial point of one vector to the terminal point of the other. It is known as triangle law of vector addition.

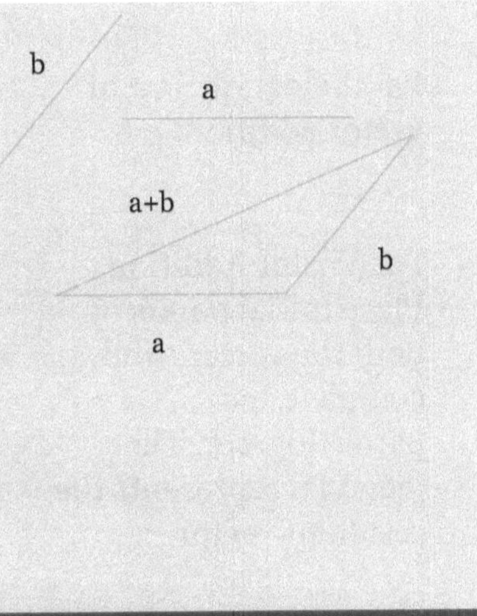

19-02-2022

Addition of Vectors

(7)

Parallelogram law of vector addition:

For Vector Addition, Place initial points of both the vectors and complete the parallelogram. The diagonal represents the resultant vector.

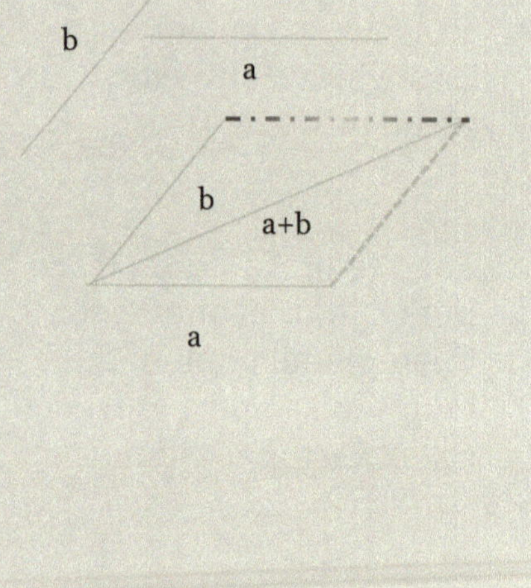

19-02-2022

Multiplication of a vector by a scalar

(8)

Scalar	x	y		0	0
1	2	3		2	3
0	2	3		0	0
0.5	2	3		1	1.5
0	2	3		0	0
5	2	3		10	15
0	2	3		0	0
-5	2	3		-10	-15
0	2	3		0	0

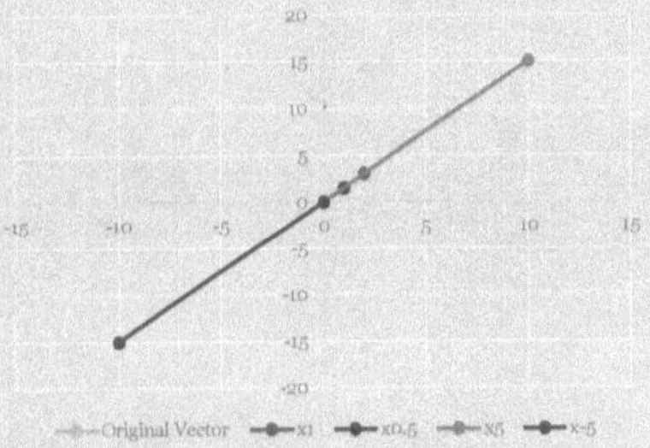

19-02-2022

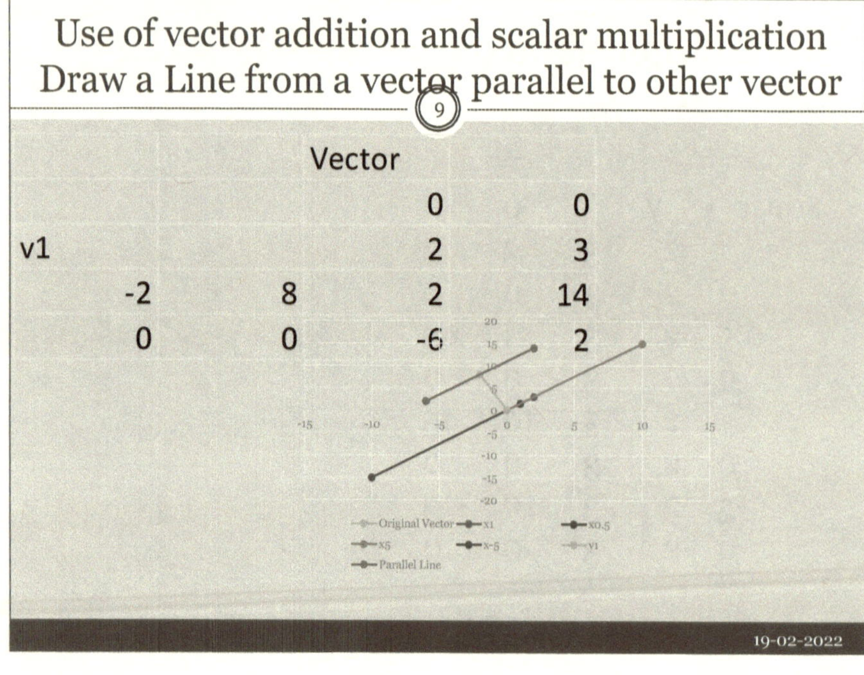
Use of vector addition and scalar multiplication
Draw a Line from a vector parallel to other vector
9
Vector
0   0
v1   2   3
-2   8   2   14
0   0   -6   2
20
15
10
5
0
-15   -10   -5   0   5   10   15
-5
-10
-15
-20
Original Vector   X1   X0.5
X5   X-5   v1
Parallel Line
19-02-2022

Draw a vector from a vector parallel to other vector

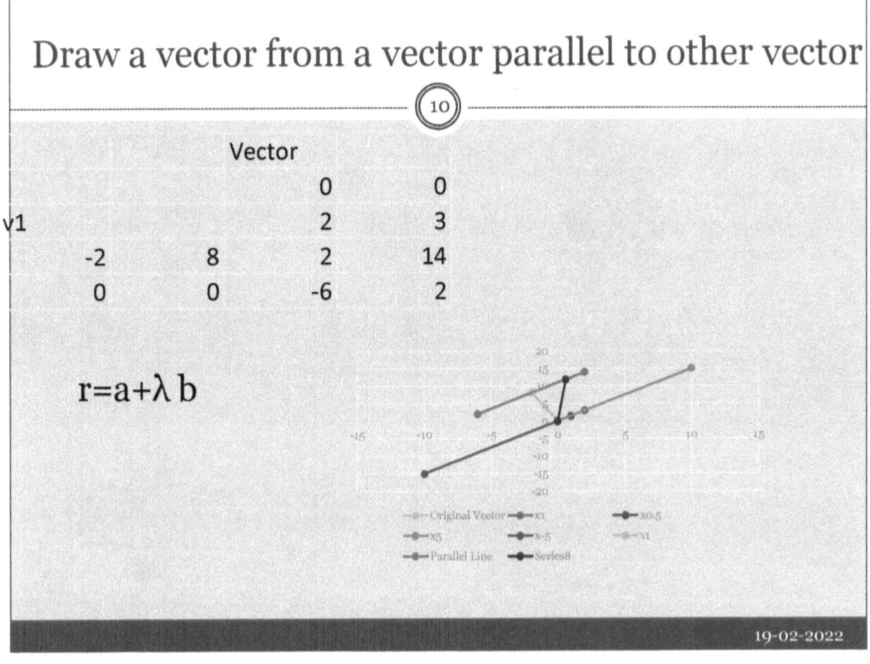

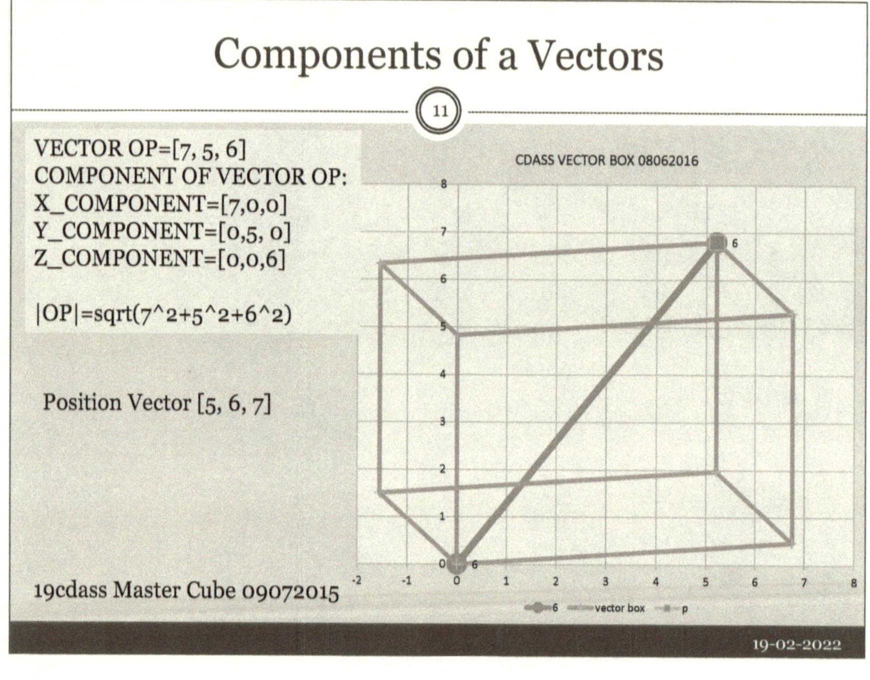
Components of a Vectors
11
VECTOR OP=[7, 5, 6]
COMPONENT OF VECTOR OP:
X_COMPONENT=[7,0,0]
Y_COMPONENT=[0,5, 0]
Z_COMPONENT=[0,0,6]

|OP|=sqrt(7^2+5^2+6^2)

Position Vector [5, 6, 7]

19cdass Master Cube 09072015
CDASS VECTOR BOX 08062016
8
7
6
5
4
3
2
1
0
-2 -1 0 1 2 3 4 5 6 7 8
6 vector box p
19-02-2022

Data for representation of a vector

	vector box	0	0	0
0	vector box	7	0	0
1	vector box	7	5	0
2	vector box	0	5	0
3	vector box	0	0	0
0	vector box	0	0	6
4	vector box	7	0	6
5	vector box	7	5	6
6	vector box	0	5	6
7	vector box	0	5	0
3	vector box	7	5	0
2	vector box	7	5	6
6	vector box	7	0	6
5	vector box	7	0	0
1	vector box	0	0	0
0	vector box	0	0	6
4	vector box	0	5	6
7				

VECTOR OP=[7, 5, 6]

19-02-2022

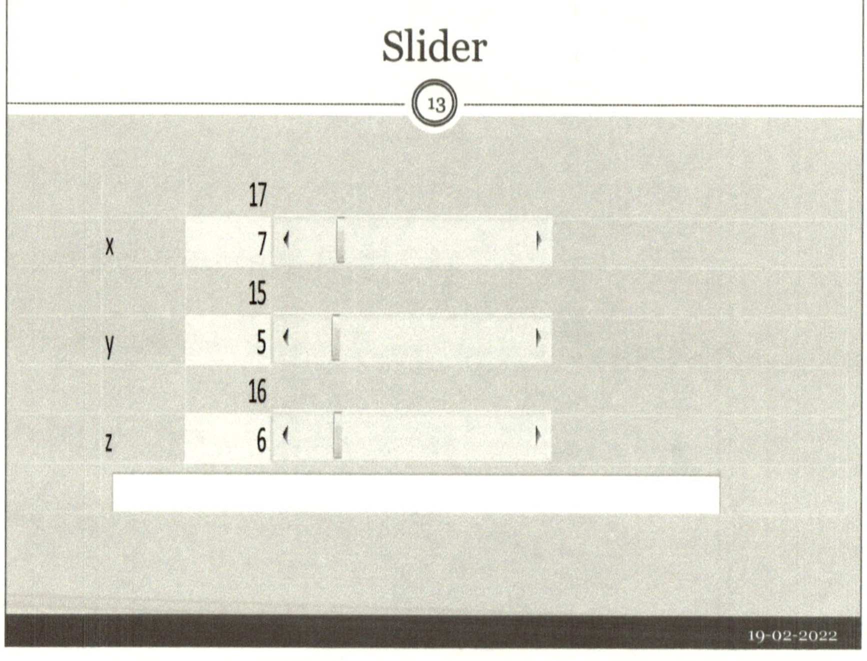
Slider
13
17
x   7
15
y   5
16
z   6
19-02-2022

Vector Joining Two Points

- $P=[x_1, y_1\ z_1]$ $Q=[x_2, y_2, z_3]$
- $PQ=P_2-P_1=[X_2-X_1, Y_2-Y_1, Z_2-Z_1]$
- $|PQ|=SQRT((X_2-X_1)^2+(Y_2-Y_1)^2+(Z_2-Z_1)^2)$

P	-3	2	6
Q	9	3	1
PQ	12	1	-5
	0	0	0

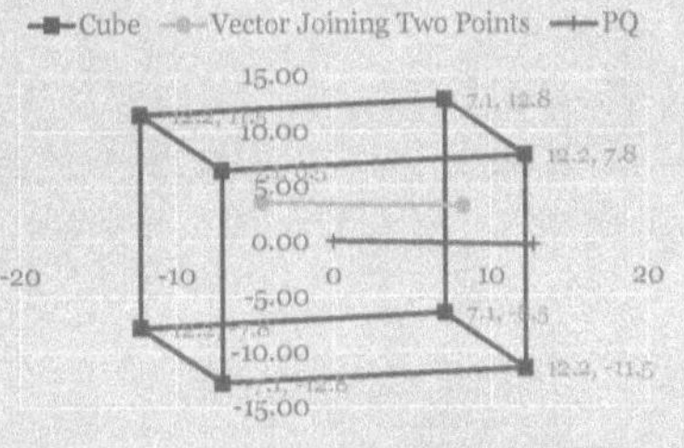

19-02-2022

Section Formula

A "ratio" is just a comparison between two different things.
Suppose there are thirty-five people, fifteen of whom are men. Then the ratio of men to women is **15 to 20**.

In **mathematics**, two variables are **proportional** if a change in one is always accompanied by a change in the other, and if the changes are always related by use of a constant multiplier. The constant is called the coefficient of proportionality or proportionality constant.

19-02-2022

Section Formula

(16)

- The **section formula** tells us the coordinates of the point which divides a given line segment into two parts such that their lengths are in the ratio m:n.

P(x1,y1) m n Q(x2,y2)

- $x = \dfrac{m\,x2 + n\,x1}{m+n}$
- $y = \dfrac{m\,y2 + n\,y1}{m+n}$

19-02-2022

SECTION FORMULA

- P=[x1, y1 z1]
- Q=[x2, y2,z3]
- Rin=[x,y] divides PQ in the ratio m:n INTERNALLY
- x= (m*X2+n*X1)/(m+n), y= (m*Y2+n*Y1)/(m+n)
- Rout=[x,y] divides PQ in the ratio m:n EXTERNALLY
- x= (m*X2-n*X1)/(m-n), y= (m*Y2-n*Y1)/(m-n)

19-02-2022

Section Formula

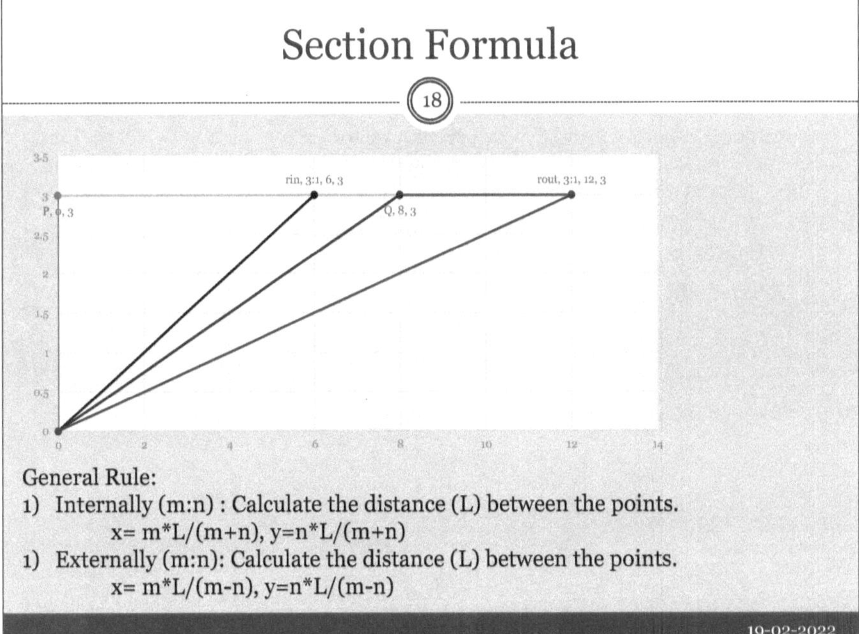

General Rule:
1) Internally (m:n) : Calculate the distance (L) between the points.
   x= m*L/(m+n), y=n*L/(m+n)
1) Externally (m:n): Calculate the distance (L) between the points.
   x= m*L/(m-n), y=n*L/(m-n)

19-02-2022

Example-11

(19)

Consider two points P and Q with position vector OP=3a-2b and OQ=a+b. Find the position vector of a point R which divides the line segment joining P & Q in the ratio 2:1 (i) internally, and (2) externally

1) Internally, $x=\dfrac{2\,(a+b)+1\,(3a-2b)}{2+1}=\dfrac{5a}{3}$

2) Externally, $x=\dfrac{2\,(a+b)-1\,(3a-2b)}{2-1}=4\ b\ \text{-a}$

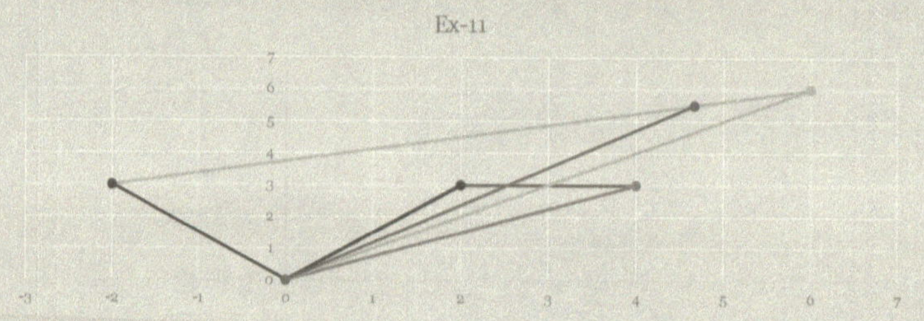

Ex-11

Section Formula for Vectors(Internally)

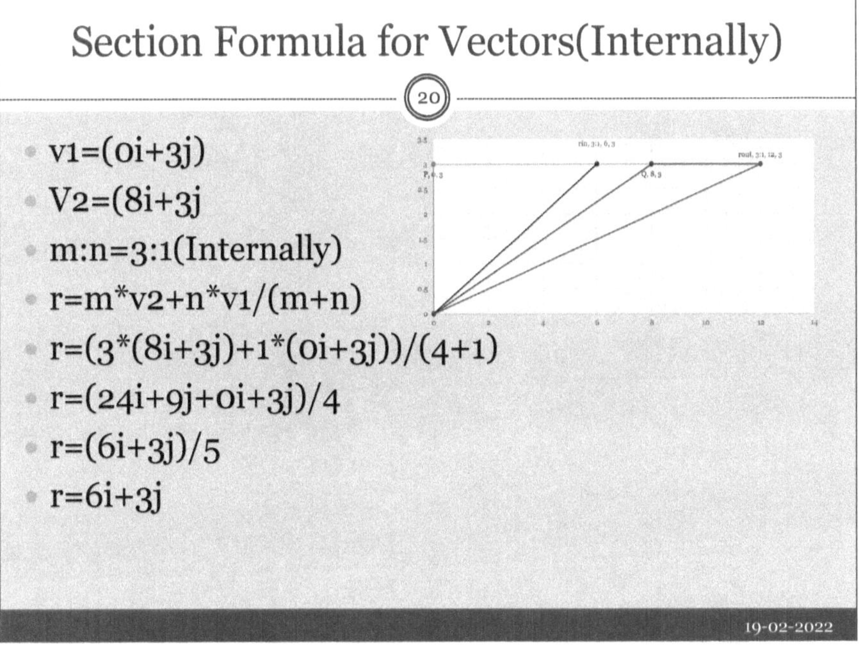

- v1=(0i+3j)
- V2=(8i+3j
- m:n=3:1(Internally)
- r=m*v2+n*v1/(m+n)
- r=(3*(8i+3j)+1*(0i+3j))/(4+1)
- r=(24i+9j+0i+3j)/4
- r=(6i+3j)/5
- r=6i+3j

19-02-2022

Section Formula for Vector(Externally)

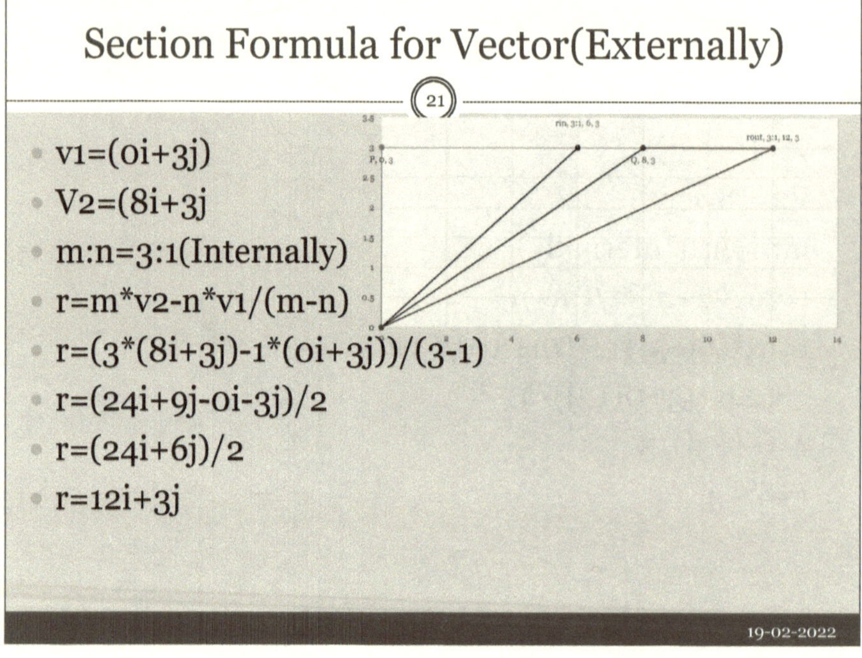

- v1=(0i+3j)
- V2=(8i+3j
- m:n=3:1(Internally)
- r=m*v2-n*v1/(m-n)
- r=(3*(8i+3j)-1*(0i+3j))/(3-1)
- r=(24i+9j-0i-3j)/2
- r=(24i+6j)/2
- r=12i+3j

19-02-2022

Direction Cosines

22

VECTOR OP=[7, 5, 6]
COMPONENT OF VECTOR OP:
X_COMPONENT=[7,0,0]
Y_COMPONENT=[0,5, 0]
Z_COMPONENT=[0,0,6]

$r=|OP|=sqrt(7^2+5^2+6^2)=10.488$

$l=\cos(\alpha)=x/r = 7/10.488$
$m=\cos(\beta) =y/r=5/10.488$
$n=\cos(\gamma) = z/r =6/10.488$

Direction ratios:
a=l r, b=m r, c=n r (r=-n to n)

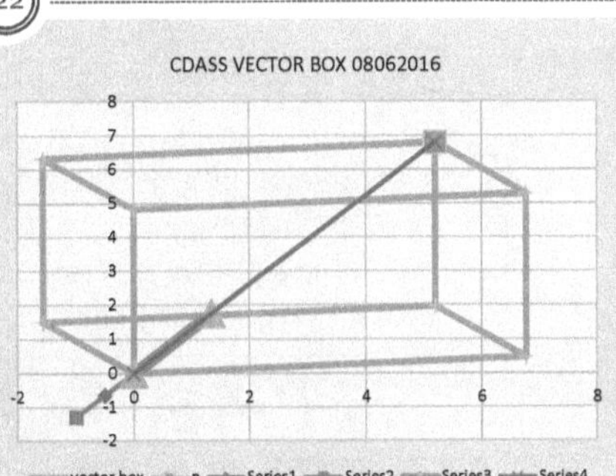

| 0.840052 | 1.073864 | 0.96176 | Radian |
| 48.13146 | 61.52787 | 55.10477 | Degree |

19-02-2022

VECTORS

(23)

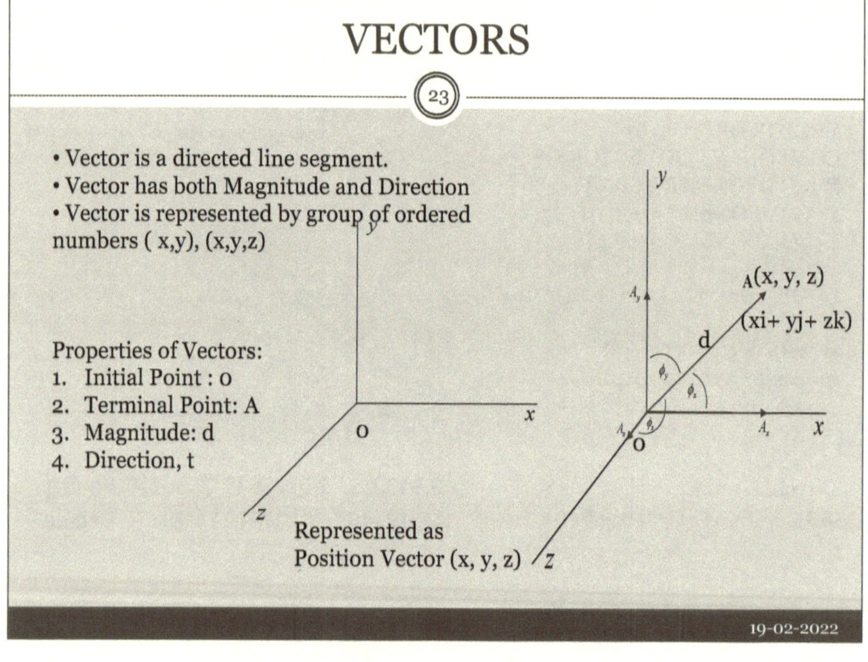

• Vector is a directed line segment.
• Vector has both Magnitude and Direction
• Vector is represented by group of ordered numbers (x,y), (x,y,z)

Properties of Vectors:
1. Initial Point : o
2. Terminal Point: A
3. Magnitude: d
4. Direction, t

Represented as
Position Vector (x, y, z)

19-02-2022

Vector vs Null Vector

- Vector, v1 = (1, 6)
- Vector, v2=(1,6,-13)
- Vector, v3=(0, 0, 0)
- Geometrically these vectors looks like:

19-02-2022

VECTORS

(25)

Vector Representation:

$$\mathbf{A} = A_x\mathbf{i} + A_y\mathbf{j} + A_z\mathbf{k}$$

$$A = (A_x, A_y, A_z)$$

(A_x, A_y, A_z are scalars)

Magnitude or Absolute Value:

$$A = |\mathbf{A}| = \sqrt{A_x^2 + A_y^2 + A_z^2}$$

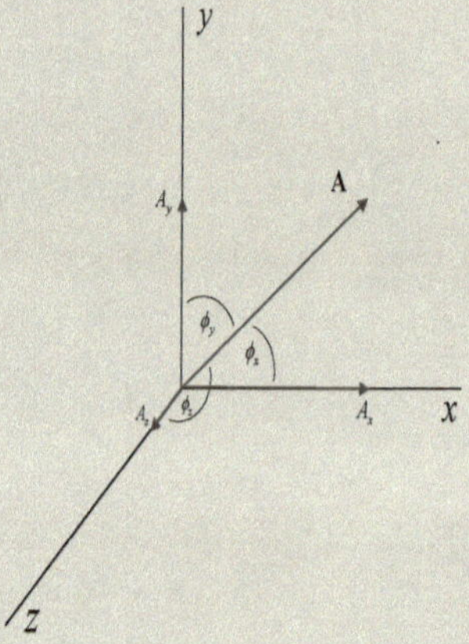

Example:

$$\mathbf{F} = 3\mathbf{i} + 4\mathbf{j} - 12\mathbf{k}$$

$$F = \sqrt{(3)^2 + (4)^2 + (-12)^2}$$

$$= 13\,\text{N}$$

19-02-2022

Vector Representation

- Vectors are represented by (x, y) in 2d and (x, y, z) in 3d
- Vectors has an initial point represented by (x1,y1) or (x1,y1,z1) and end point (x2,y2) or (x2,y2,z2).

- Then how the vectors represented by (x,y) or (x,y,z)

- Example: Point A=(2, 5), B=(5,9).
- What is the vector AB?

19-02-2022

Vector Representation

(27)

- Example: Point a=(2, 5), b=(5,6).
- What is the vector ab?
- Answer: The given vector is (5-2),(6-5)) =(3, 1)
- The given vectors are shown below:

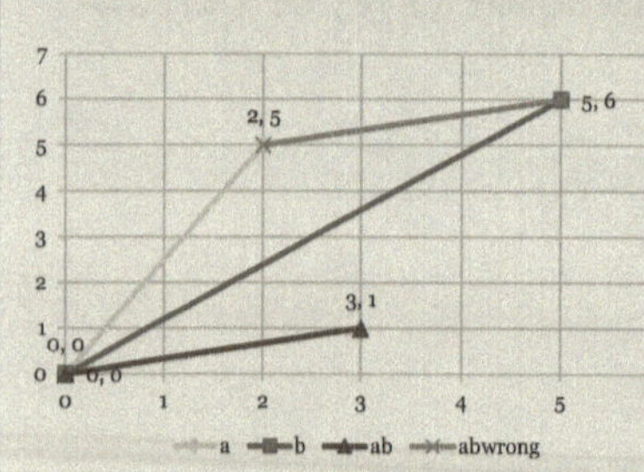

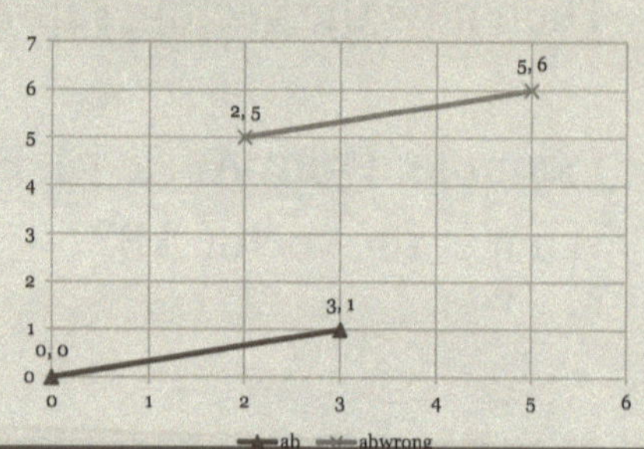

19-02-2022

Vector in 3d

(28)

P=(5, 3, 7)
P=(5i+3j+7k)

Q=(7, 1, 1)
Q=(7i+j+k)

PQ=(2i+2j+6k)

- Vector PQ
  =(5-7, 3-1, 7-1)= (-2, 2, 6)

- PQ=(5-7)i+(3-1)j+(7-1)k= -2i+2j+6k

- What is the Initial Point of PQ??

19-02-2022

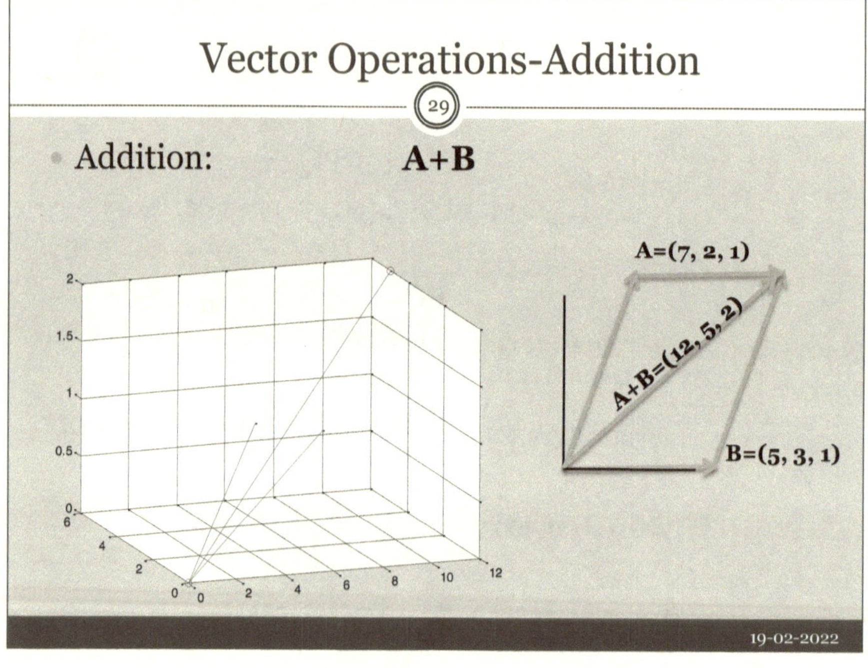
Vector Operations-Addition
29
Addition: A+B
A=(7, 2, 1)
A+B=(12, 5, 2)
B=(5, 3, 1)
19-02-2022

Scalar Multiplication

(30)

- Multiplication of a vector by a scalar: 2*C
- =2*(6,4,2)
- =(12,8,4)
- Scalar multiplication of a vector, makes it larger and smaller.
- This is a major topic in eigen value problems.

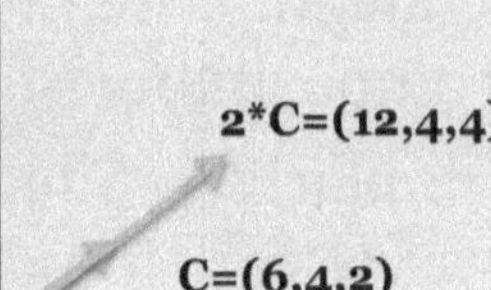

19-02-2022

Product of two vectors

- Points to remember:
- Product of two numbers is a number.
- Product of two matrices is a matrix
- Functions are multiplied in two ways-elementwise or compositionwise.
- Similarly, product of two vectors are done in two ways-scalar product and vector product.

19-02-2022

Vector Operations-Dot Product

(32)

- $A=[xa, ya, za]$, $B=[xb, yb, zb]$
- Scalar or Dot Product: **A•B**
  $a.b = xa*xb + ya*yb + za*zb$

$$(7 \quad 2 \quad 1) * \begin{pmatrix} 5 \\ 3 \\ 1 \end{pmatrix} = 7*5 + 2*3 + 1*1 = 42$$

Result is a Scalar

Multiply Column-wise and then add
7 2 1
5 3 1
35 +6+1 = 42

19-02-2022

Dot Product (Output is Scalar)

(33)

Definition:

$$\mathbf{A} \bullet \mathbf{B} = AB \cos\theta$$

Computation:

$$\mathbf{A} \bullet \mathbf{B} = A_x B_x + A_y B_y + A_z B_z$$

$$A.B = \begin{bmatrix} 2 & 3 & 2 \end{bmatrix} \begin{bmatrix} 5 \\ 7 \\ 1 \end{bmatrix} = \left[2\times 5 + 3\times 7 + 2\times 1 \right] = 33$$

(2i+3j+2k).(5i+7j+1k)=10i^2+15 ij+10kj+14ij+21j^2+14kj+2 ik+3 jk+2 k^2
=10 i^2+21 j^2+2 k^2 =10+21+2=33
As ij=jk=ki=ik=kj=ji=0 and i^2=j^2=k^2=1

$$(2i+3j+2k).(5i+7j+1k) = (10i^2 + 21j^2 + 2k^2) = 33$$

$$(\because i^2 = j^2 = k^2 = 1)$$

Note: Because cos 0=1, cos 90 = 0

B(5, 7, 1)

θ

A(2, 3, 2)

19-02-2022

Geometrical Interpretation of Dot Product

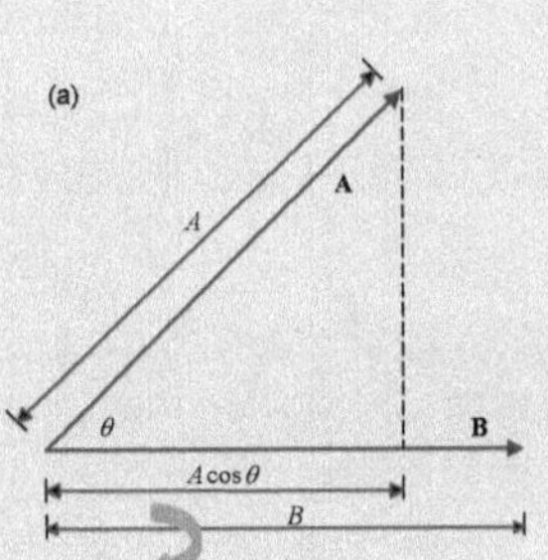

Projection of **A** on **B**
Projection of A on B=|A| cos(t)

19-02-2022

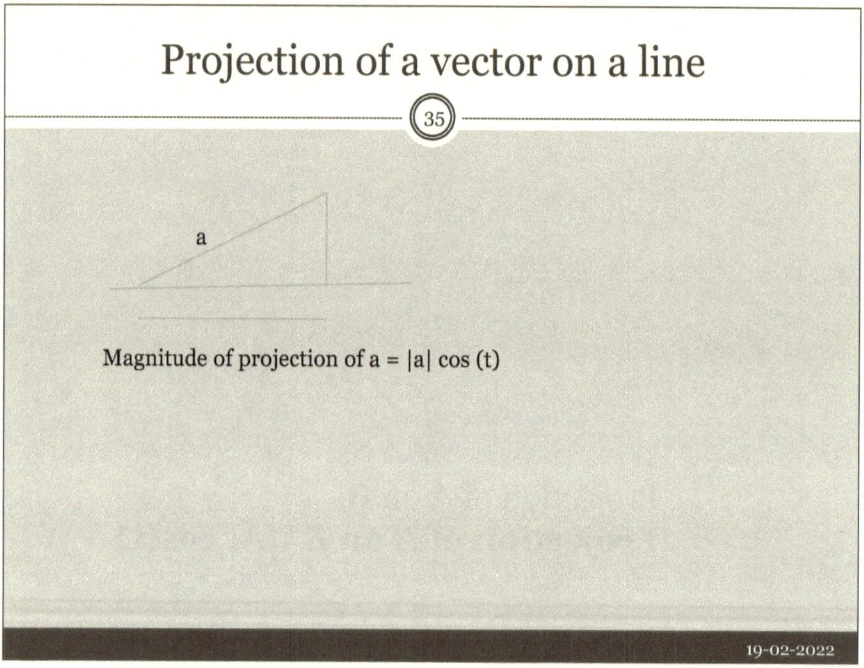

Projection of a vector on a line

(35)

a

Magnitude of projection of a = |a| cos (t)

19-02-2022

Projection of a vector on a vector

a

Magnitude of projection of a = |a| cos (t)

We know that a.b=|a|.|b| cos(t)
 or Magnitude of Projection of a on b, |a| cos(t) = a.b/|b|

The projection vector of a on b is p=a.b/|b|*b/|b|

Basis: Unit vector in the direction of b and dot product of a and unit vector in direction of b

19-02-2022

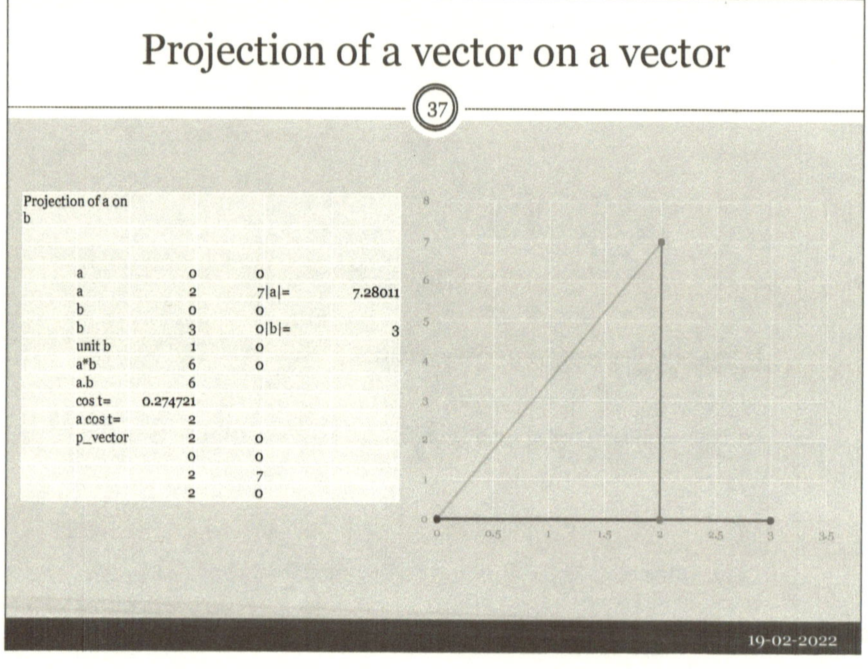

Projection of a vector on a vector
37
Projection of a on b

a	0	0
a	2	7|a|=	7.28011
b	0	0
b	3	0|b|=	3
unit b	1	0
a*b	6	0
a.b	6
cos t=	0.274721
a cos t=	2
p_vector	2	0
	0	0
	2	7
	2	0

19-02-2022

Projection of a vector on a vector

(38)

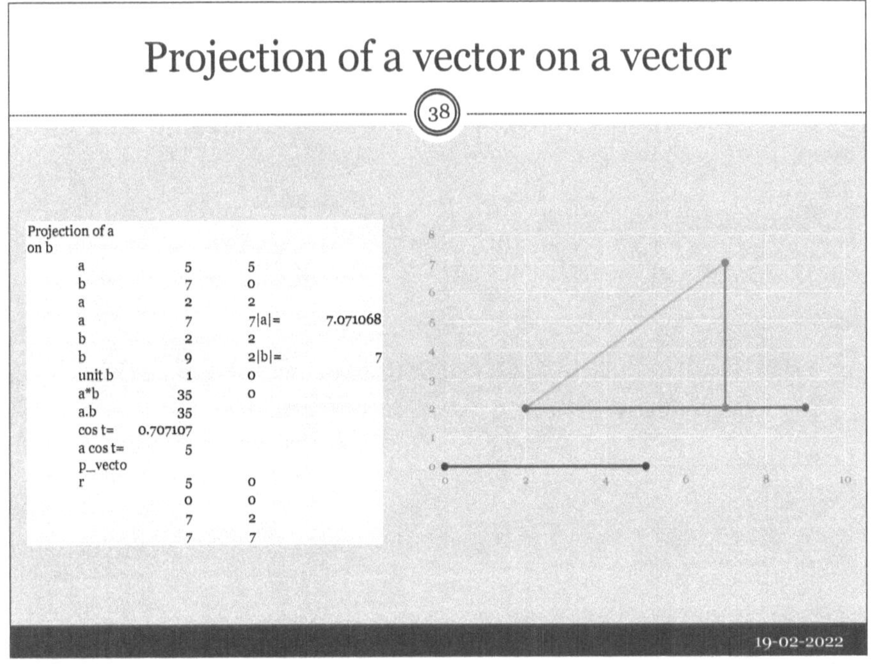

Projection of a on b				
a	5	5		
b	7	0		
a	2	2		
a	7	7|a|=	7.071068
b	2	2		
b	9	2|b|=	7
unit b	1	0		
a*b	35	0		
a.b	35			
cos t=	0.707107			
a cos t=	5			
p_vecto r	5	0		
	0	0		
	7	2		
	7	7		

Finding Unit Vector

- Let v=xi+yj+zk
- Then $|v|$=sqrt(x^2+y^2+z^2)
- Unit Vector v = xi/$|v|$+yj/$|v|$+zk/$|v|$

- Unit vector is required for calculating Cross Product of Two Vector, finding projection vector, etc.

19-02-2022

Finding Angle between two vectors from Dot Product

Step-1: Find the Magnitude of both the vectors.
Step-2: Find the dot product of the vectors
Step-3: Calculate cos(t)=A.B/|A|*|B| =x
Step-4: Calculate t=acos(x)

(a)

To calculate Projection of A on B, A cos (t) use the formula
cos(t)=A.B/|A|*|B|
Or |A| cos(t) = A.B/|B|

To find the coordinates of Projection Vector,

V=A.B/|B|*B/|B|

Chanchal Dass, FIE, Email: cdass01@gmail.com, Mobile: +91-8320172787

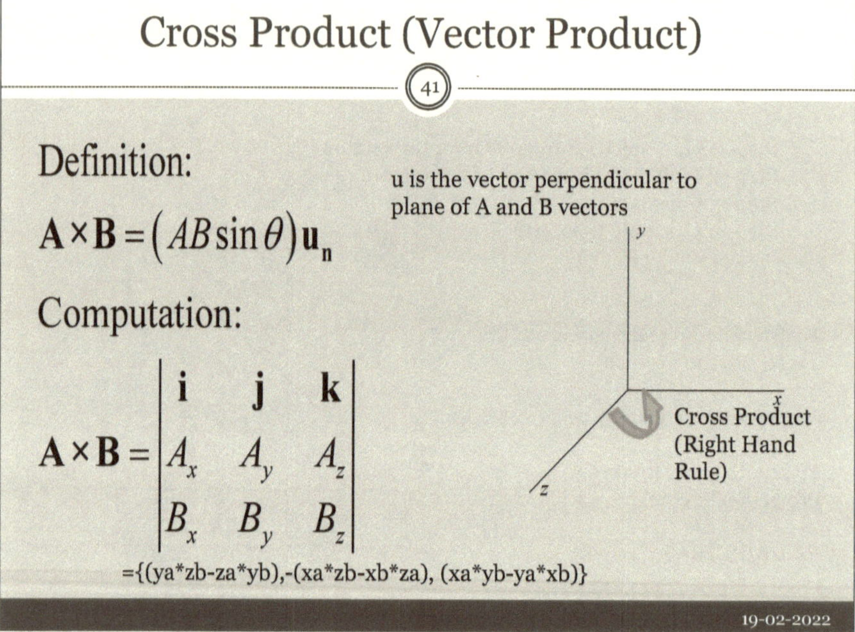
Cross Product (Vector Product)
41
Definition:
$$\mathbf{A} \times \mathbf{B} = \left(AB \sin\theta \right) \mathbf{u_n}$$
Computation:
$$\mathbf{A} \times \mathbf{B} = \begin{vmatrix} \mathbf{i} & \mathbf{j} & \mathbf{k} \\ A_x & A_y & A_z \\ B_x & B_y & B_z \end{vmatrix}$$
={(ya*zb-za*yb),-(xa*zb-xb*za), (xa*yb-ya*xb)}
u is the vector perpendicular to plane of A and B vectors
y
x
z
Cross Product
(Right Hand
Rule)
19-02-2022

Computation of Cross Product

(42)

$$\mathbf{A} \times \mathbf{B} = \begin{vmatrix} \mathbf{i} & \mathbf{j} & \mathbf{k} \\ A_x & A_y & A_z \\ B_x & B_y & B_z \end{vmatrix} = \begin{vmatrix} \mathbf{i} & \mathbf{j} & \mathbf{k} \\ 2 & -2 & 1 \\ 3 & 4 & 12 \end{vmatrix}$$

A= (2, -2, 1), B=(3, 4, 12)

$$\mathbf{A} \times \mathbf{B} = \left[(-2)(12) - (1)(4)\right]\mathbf{i} - \left[(2)(12) - (1)(3)\right]\mathbf{j}$$
$$+ \left[(2)(4) - (-2)(3)\right]\mathbf{k}$$
$$= -28\mathbf{i} - 21\mathbf{j} + 14\mathbf{k}$$

AXB=[-28, -21, 14]

19-02-2022

Vector Cross Product

* AxB=|A| |B|sin (t) n (n=unit vector along normal)

Observations:
1. axb is a vector
2. axb is 0 iff the two vectors are parallel or collinear
3. If t=90 then axb=|a||b|n
4. ixi=jxj=kxk=0 and ixj=k, jxk=i, kxi=j
5. sin(t)=|axb|/|a||b|
6. ixj#jxi

19-02-2022

Finding Area of a Triangle

- AxB=|A| |B|sin (t) n (n=unit vector along normal)

Observations:

7. Area of the triangle formed by the vectors as adjacent sides is ½*|axb|=1/2*|a||b||sin(t)

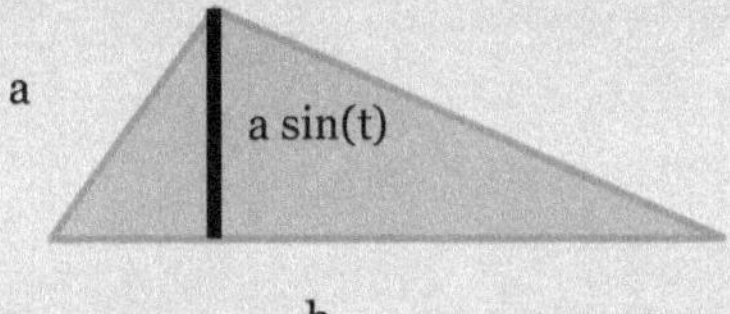

From the formula:
Area=1/2 base x Height

19-02-2022

Vector Product

- AxB=|A| |B|sin (t) n (n=unit vector along normal)

Observations:

7. Area of the parallelogram formed by the vectors as adjacent sides is |axb|=|a||b||sin(t)

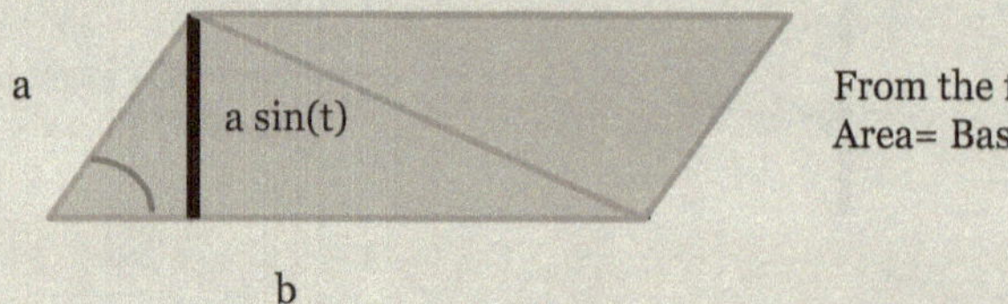

19-02-2022

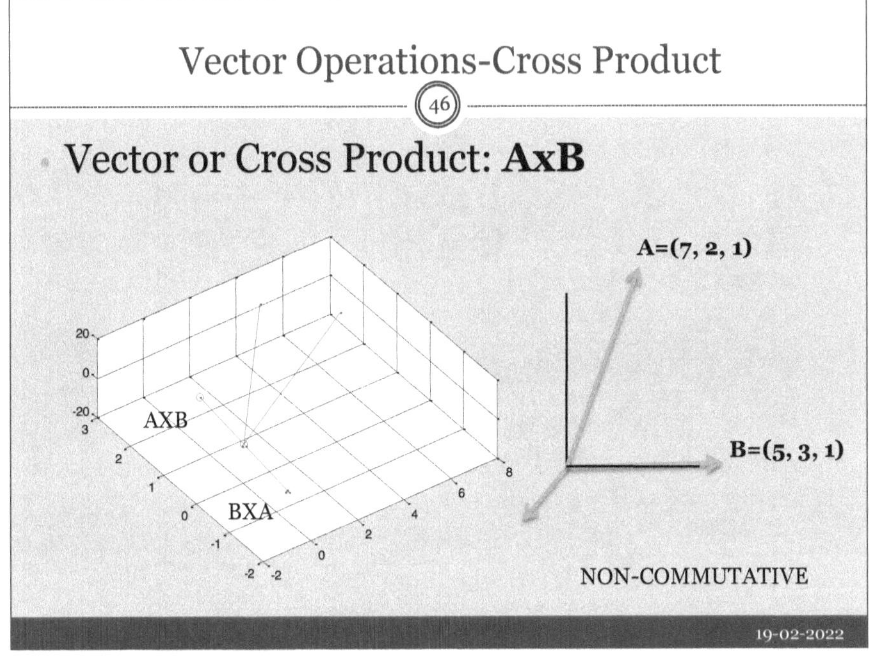

Vector Operations-Cross Product
46
Vector or Cross Product: AxB
A=(7, 2, 1)
B=(5, 3, 1)
AXB
BXA
NON-COMMUTATIVE
19-02-2022

Scalar Triple Product

(47)

- Triple Scalar Product: $(AxB) \cdot C$
- $=(7, 2, 1)X(5,3,1).(6,4,2)$
- $=(-1,-2,11).(6,4,2)$
- $=8$
- **This triple product will generate a scalar equal to the volume of the parallelepiped formed by the vectors**

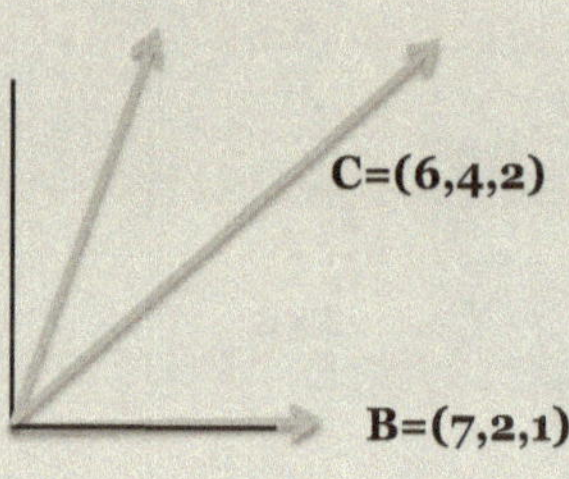

19-02-2022

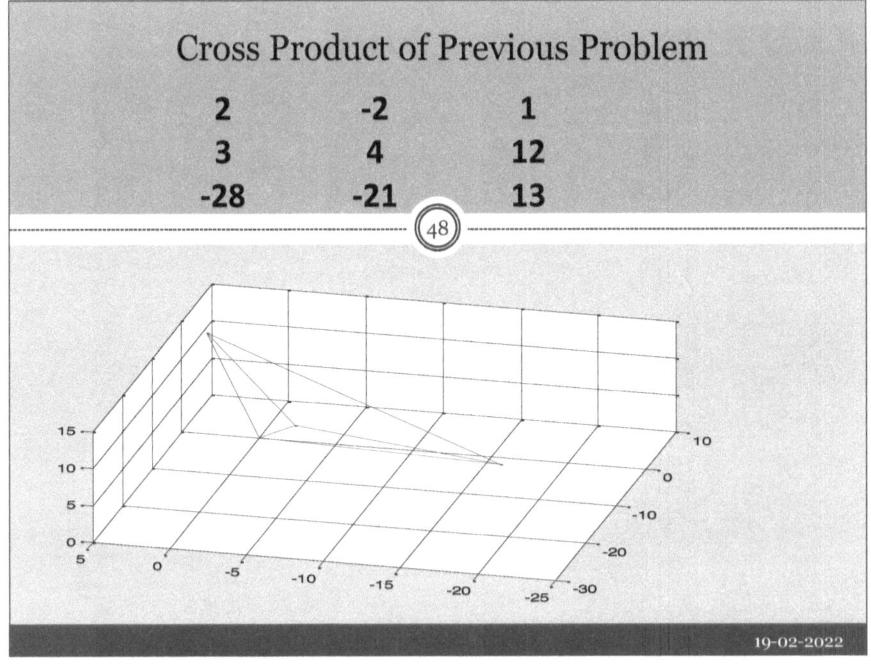

Cross Product of Previous Problem
2   -2   1
3   4   12
-28   -21   13
48
15
10
5
0
5
0
-5
-10
-15
-20
-25
-30
-20
-10
0
10
19-02-2022

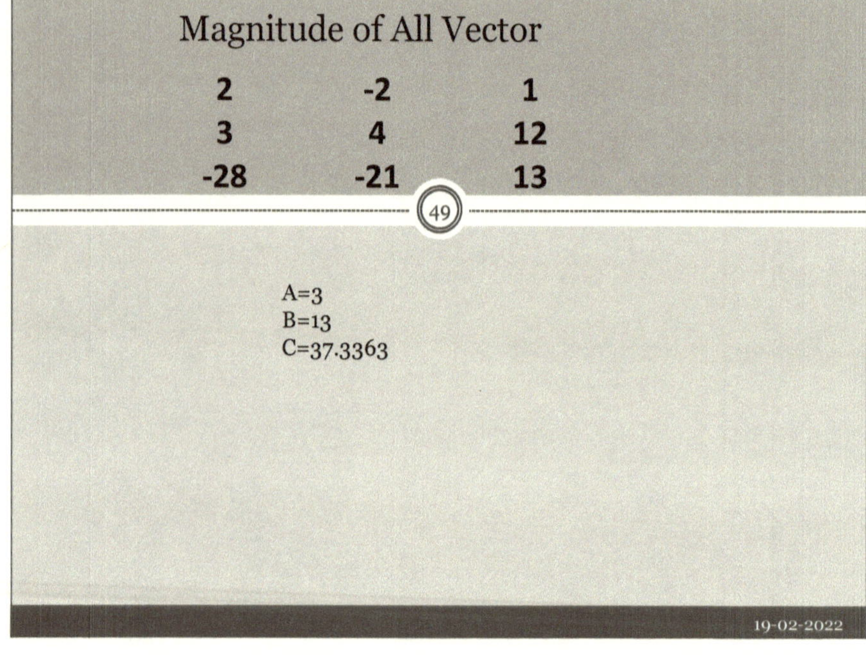
Magnitude of All Vector
2   -2   1
3   4   12
-28   -21   13
49
A=3
B=13
C=37.3363
19-02-2022

Dot and Cross Product Formulas

xa	ya	za
2	3	1
xb	yb	zb
3	5	2

$$a.b = xa*xb + ya*yb = 21$$

$$a.b = xa*xb + ya*yb + za*zb = 23$$

$$Axb = (x,y,z)$$
$$= \{(ya*zb - za*yb), -((xa*zb - xb*za), (xa*yb - ya*xb)\} = (1,-1,1)$$

19-02-2022

Angle from Dot Product

(51)

Dot Product of two vectors A and B gives the angle formed by the vectors with MATLAB command

```
a=[2,3,1]
b=[3,5,2]
ab=[b(1)-a(1), b(2)-a(2), b(3)-a(3)]
adotb=dot(a,b)
axb=cross(a,b)
plot3([0,a(1)],[0,a(2)],[0,a(3)])
hold on
plot3([0,b(1)],[0,b(2)],[0,b(3)])
plot3([0,ab(1)],[0,ab(2)1],[0,ab(3)])
grid
absa=norm(a)
absb=norm(b)
angle=acos((adotb)/(absa*absb))
t=angle*180/pi
```

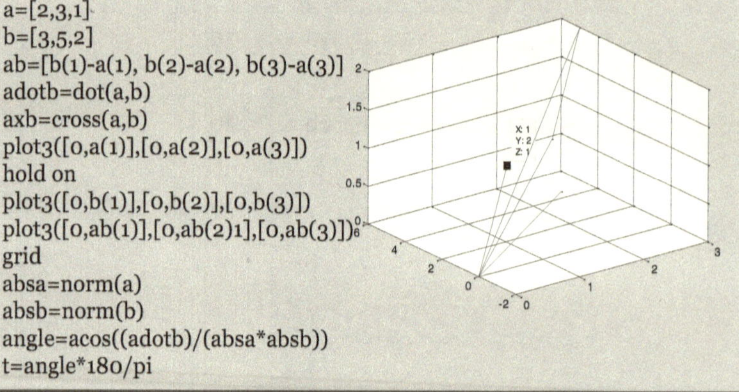

19-02-2022

Angle from Dot Product

Dot Product of two vectors A and B gives the angle formed by the vectors with MATLAB command

```
a=[2,3,1]                              a =    2    3    1
b=[3,5,2]                              b =    3    5    2
ab=[b(1)-a(1), b(2)-a(2), b(3)-a(3)]   ab =   1    2    1
adotb=dot(a,b)                         adotb =   23
axb=cross(a,b)                         axb = 1   -1   1
plot3([0,a(1)],[0,a(2)],[0,a(3)])      absa =    3.7417
hold on                                absb =    6.1644
plot3([0,b(1)],[0,b(2)],[0,b(3)])      angle =   0.0752
plot3([0,ab(1)],[0,ab(2)1],[0,ab(3)])  t =    4.3066
grid
absa=norm(a)
absb=norm(b)
angle=acos((adotb)/(absa*absb))
t=angle*180/pi
```

19-02-2022

Projection of a vector on a line

(53)

If the vector **a** makes an angle t with the directed line in anticlockwise direction then the projection vector of a on l is
a*cos(t)

a

a cos (t)

Observation: Projection of a vector a on vector b is
|a| cos(t)=a.b/|b|

Now, if t =0, then va=a, if t=180, then va=-a, if t=pi/2, or
t=3pi/2, va=0

19-02-2022

Example-16

- Find the projection of a vector a = 2i+3j+2k on the vector b=i+2j+k
- The projection of vector a, |a|cos(t)=a.b/|b|

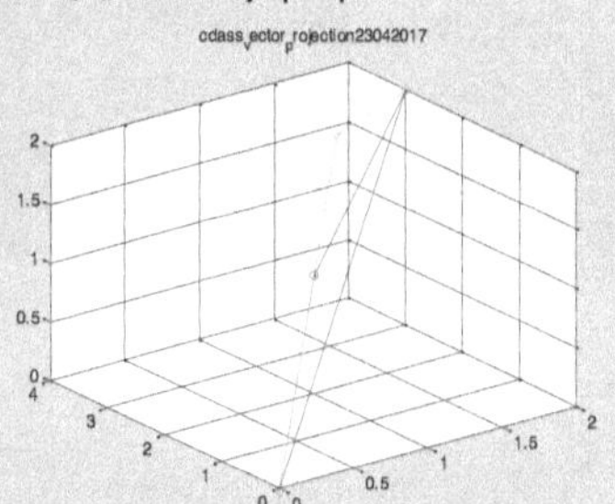

- Projection vector of a on b
- |a| cos(t)*[b/|b|]
- =(a.b/|b|)*[b/|b|]

19-02-2022

Example-16

(55)

- Find the projection of a vector a = 2i+3j+2k on the vector b=i+2j+k
- The projection of vector a, |a|cos(t)=a.b/|b|

- Projection vector of a on b
- |a| cos(t)*[b/|B|]

- =(a.b/|b|)*[b/|b|]

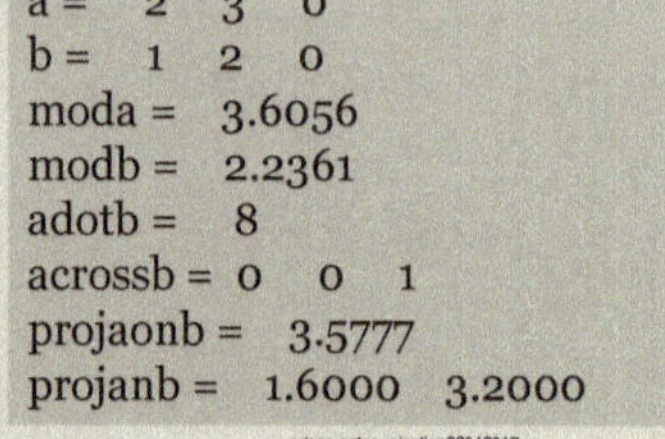

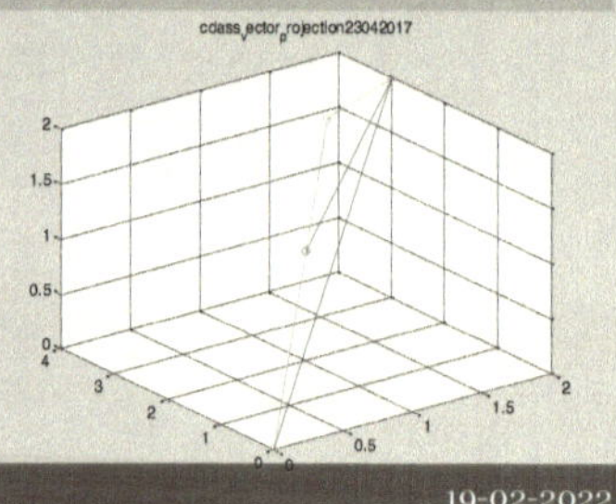

19-02-2022

Magnitude of vectors

$$|a.b| >= |a|*|b|$$

a=[2,3,1]
b=[3,5,2]
|a|=3.741
|b|=6.165
a.b=23
|a|*|b|=23.06

19-02-2022

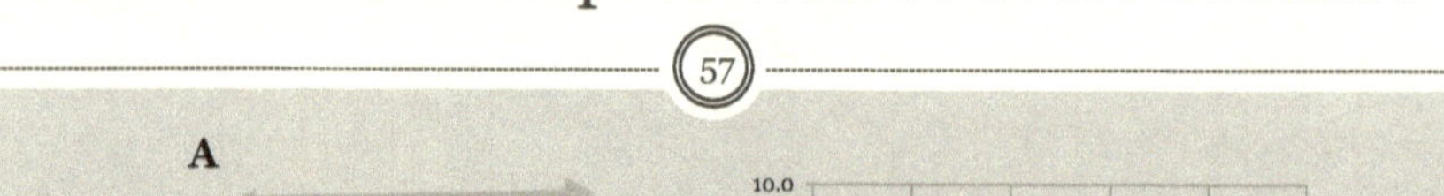

Geometrical Interpretation of Cross Product

(57)

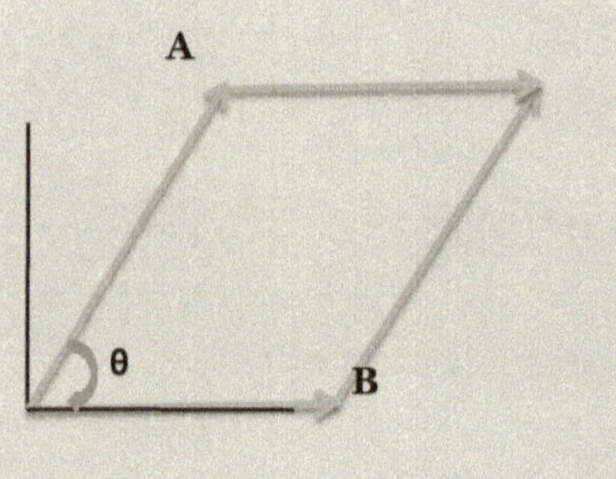

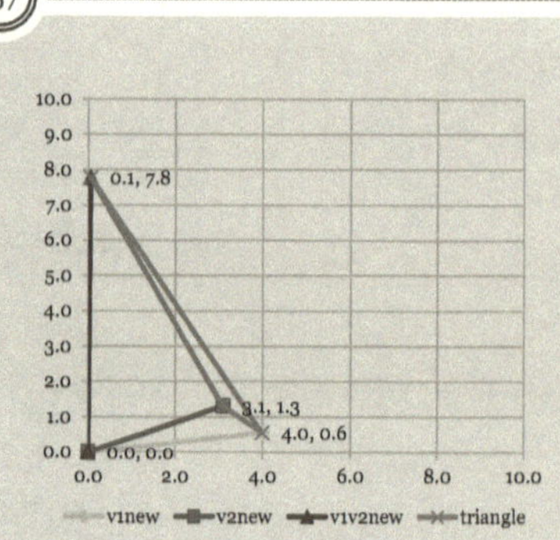

Cross Product of two vectors A and B gives the value of area
of parallelogram formed by A and B as adjacent sides

19-02-2022

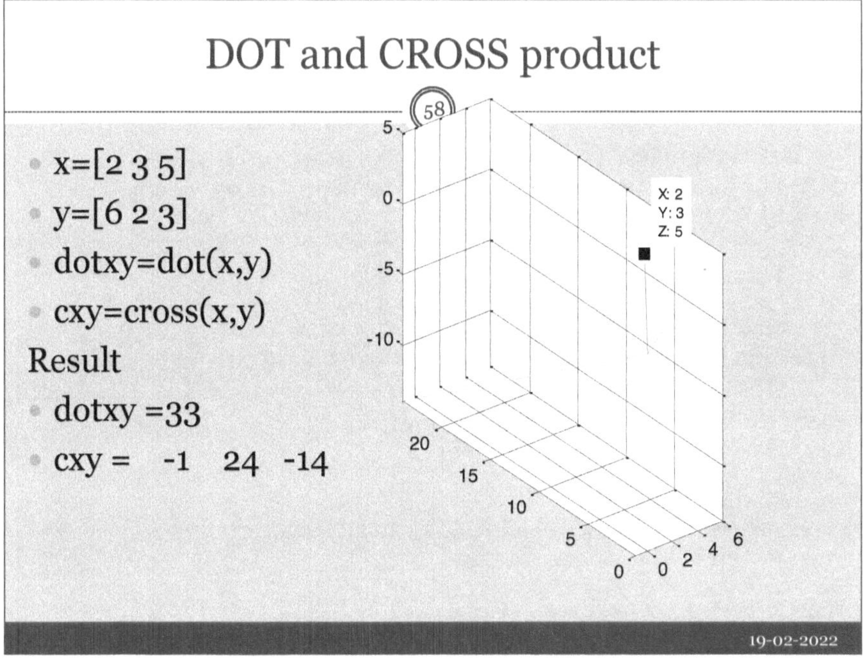
DOT and CROSS product
58
x=[2 3 5]
y=[6 2 3]
dotxy=dot(x,y)
cxy=cross(x,y)
Result
dotxy =33
cxy =   -1   24   -14
X: 2
Y: 3
Z: 5
5
0
-5
-10
20
15
10
5
0
0
2
4
6
19-02-2022

How Vector Product Finds Area?

(59)

- Important note:
- Vector product axb is only defined when a=(a1,a2,a3) and b = (b1,b2,b3) have three elements or three dimension vectors
- axb=(a2b3-a3b2, a3b1-a1b3, a1b2-a2b1)
- |axb|^2=(a2b3-a3b2)^2+(a3b1-a1b3)^2+ (a1b2-a2b1)^2
- |axb|^2=a2^2 b3^2 +a3^2 b2^2-2*a2a3b2b3+a3^2b1^2+a1^2b3^2-2a1a3b1b3+a1^2 b2^2 +a2^2 b1^2-2a1a2b1b2
- |axb|^2=(a1^2+a2^2+a3^2)(b1^2+b2^2+b3^2)-(a1b1+a2b2+a3b3)^2
- |axb|^2 =|a|^2||b|^2-(a.b)^2
- |axb|^2 =|a|^2||b|^2-|a|^2|b|^2 cos(t)^2
- |axb|^2 =|a|^2||b|^2 (1-cos(t)^2)
- |axb|^2 =|a|^2||b|^2 sin(t)^2)
- |axb|=|a||b|sin(t)
- axb is a vector perpendicular to a and b and its length is |axb|=|a||b|sin(t)

19-02-2022

Finding the Area

- We can find the area of the quadrilateral formed by the vectors a and b.

- Area=|axb|=|a||b|sin(t)

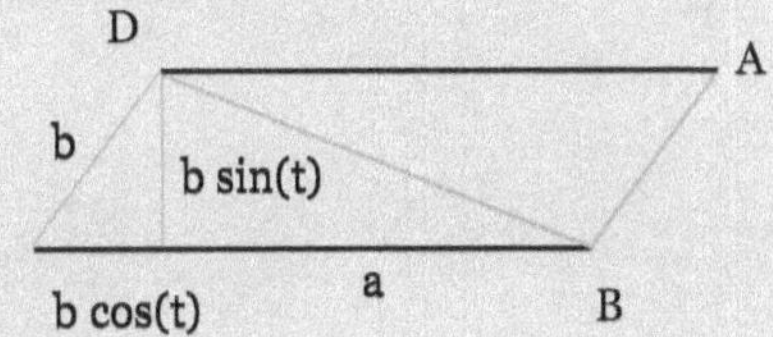

- Area of a rectangle=Length x Height
- In ABCD, Length=|a|, Height=|b| sin(t)

19-02-2022

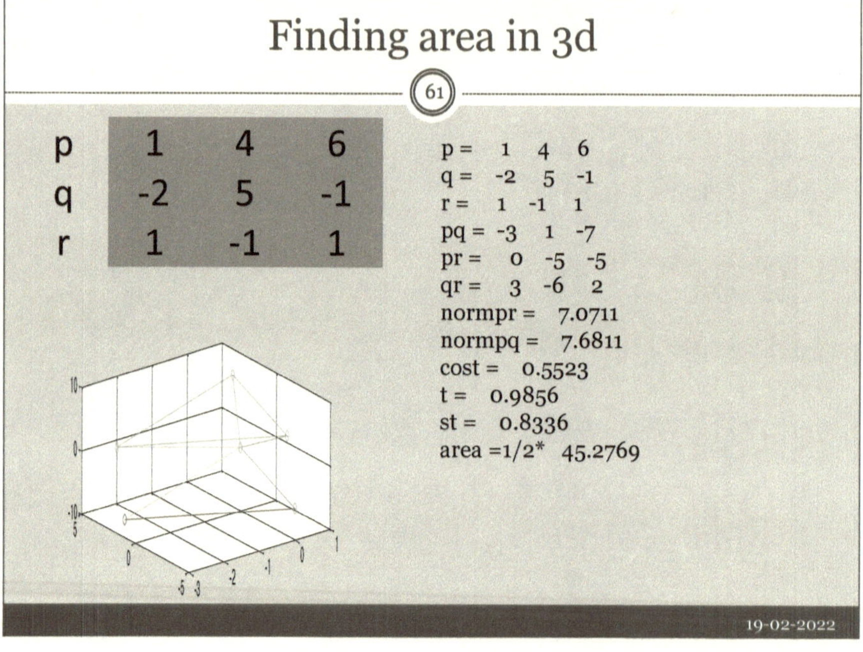
Finding area in 3d
61

p   1   4   6
q   -2   5   -1
r   1   -1   1

p =   1   4   6
q =   -2   5   -1
r =   1 -1   1
pq = -3   1   -7
pr =   0 -5   -5
qr =   3 -6   2
normpr =   7.0711
normpq =   7.6811
cost =   0.5523
t =   0.9856
st =   0.8336
area =1/2*   45.2769

19-02-2022

Example-22

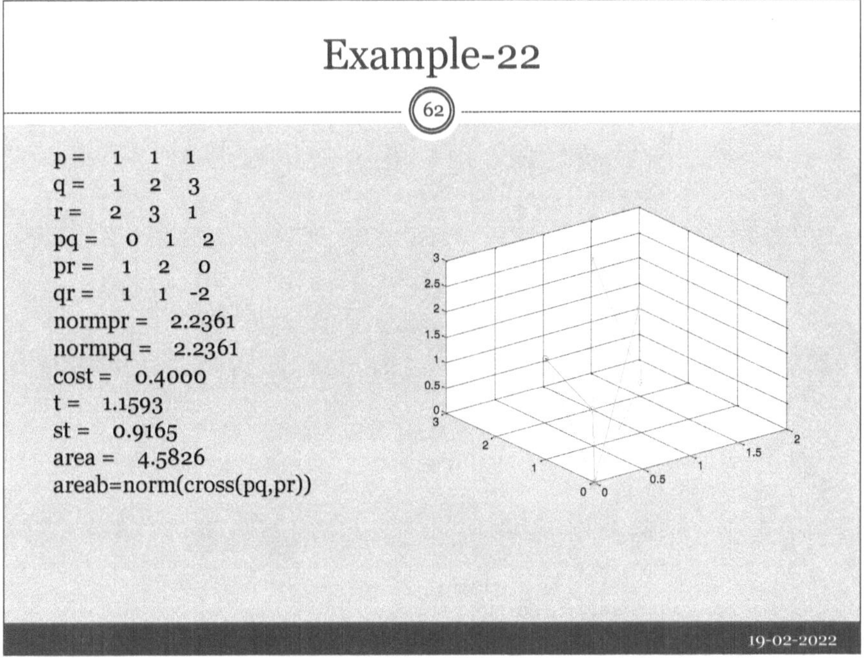

```
p =    1    1    1
q =    1    2    3
r =    2    3    1
pq =   0    1    2
pr =   1    2    0
qr =   1    1   -2
normpr =   2.2361
normpq =   2.2361
cost =   0.4000
t =    1.1593
st =   0.9165
area =   4.5826
areab=norm(cross(pq,pr))
```

Finding Volume

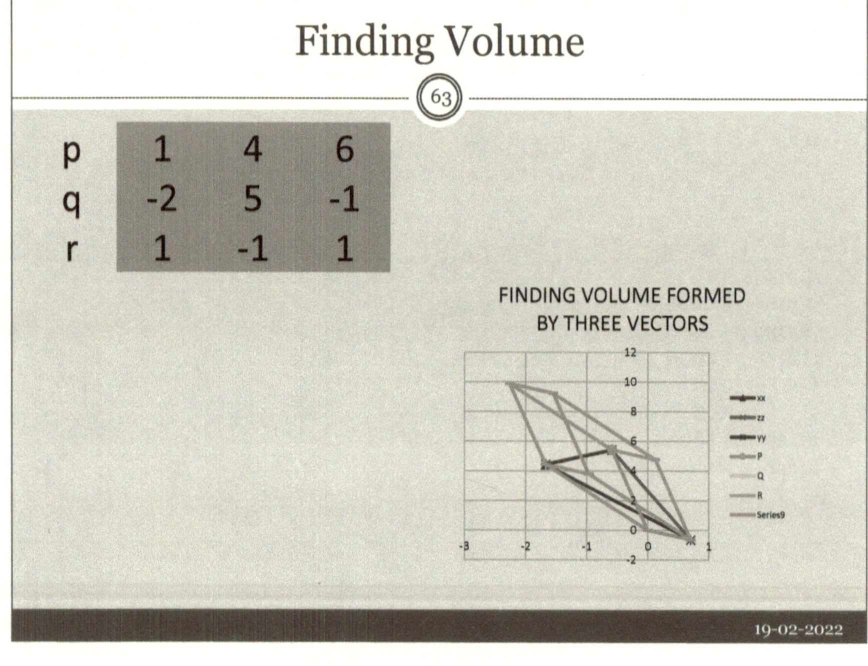

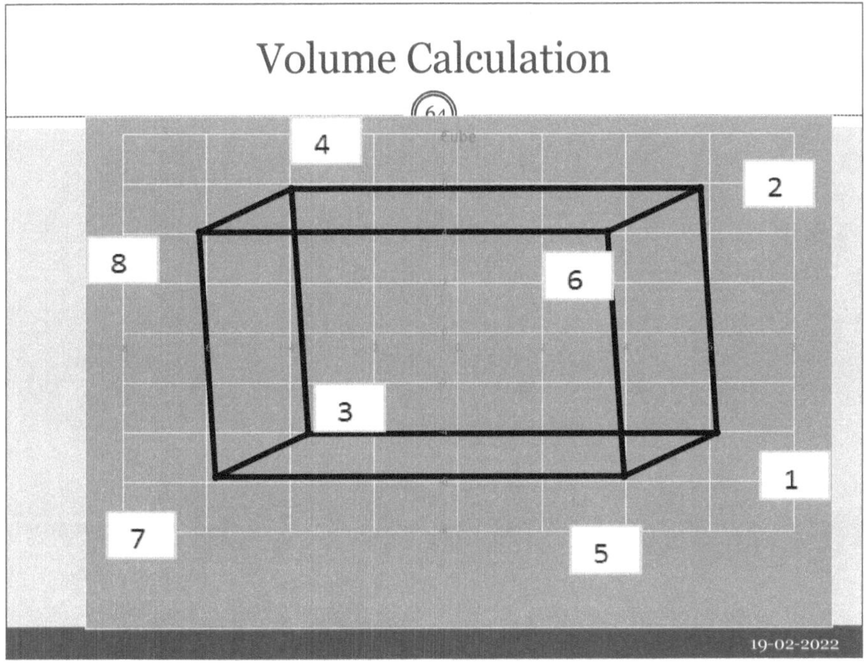
Volume Calculation
Cube
4
2
8
6
3
1
7
5
19-02-2022

Volume Calculation

(65)

P=8	1	4	6
Q=5	-2	5	-1
R=3	1	-1	1
O=7	0	0	0
4=3+8	2	4	7
1=3+5	-1	4	0
2=1+8	0	8	8
6=5+8	-1	9	5

There are eight vertex in a cube. Four Vertex are given. We have to calculate the coordinates of remaining vertices

7	0	0	0	1
5	-2	5	-1	1
6	-1	9	5	1
8	1	4	6	1
7	0	0	0	1
3	1	-1	1	1
1	-1	4	0	1
2	0	8	6	1
4	2	3	7	1
8	1	4	6	1
6	-1	9	5	1
2	0	8	6	1
1	-1	4	0	1
5	-2	5	-1	1
7	0	0	0	1
3	1	-1	1	1
4	2	3	7	1

19-02-2022

Torque

- Stewart Page 758: Ex-6:
- Force=40 NEWTON at 75 degree
- Distance= .25 m

- Here, magnitude of force and distance given.

- We know that magnitude of torque = $|t|=|r||f|\sin(t)$
- $|t|=40*.25*\sin(75)=9.66$ N.m (It is a scalar)
- Torque is $|t|$*unit vector in the direction of perpendicular to page.

19-02-2022

Three Dimensional Geometry and Vectors

67

- In dealing with 3 dimensional geometry with Cartesian coordinate system, many time, it becomes difficult to analyse. Use of Vector makes the study simple and more effective.

- Topics covered:
  1. Direction cosines and direction ratios of a line
  2. Direction cosines and direction ratios of a line joining two points
  3. Equation of lines
  4. Equation of Planes
  5. Distance between lines
  6. Distance between a point and a plane

19-02-2022

Direction Ratios

- Direction ratios provide a convenient way of specifying the direction of a line in three dimensional space.
- Direction cosines are the cosines of the angles between a line and the coordinate axes.
- Given a vector r = ai + bj + ck, its direction ratios are a : b : c.
- This means that to move in the direction of the vector we must move a units in the x direction and b units in the y direction for every c units in the z direction.

19-02-2022

Direction cosines as l m n

- If a directed line passing through origin and makes angle α, β, γ with x, y, z axis then these angles are called direction angles and cosine of these angles

$\cos(\alpha)$, $\cos(\beta)$ and $\cos(\gamma)$ are called direction cosines.

- If we reverse the direction of the line, then the direction cosines will be

$\cos(\pi + \alpha)$, $\cos(\pi + \beta)$ and $\cos(\pi + \gamma)$ and

$-\cos(\alpha)$, $-\cos(\beta)$ and $-\cos(\gamma)$.

- As same line should not have two direction ratios, we take l, m, n as direction cosines.

19-02-2022

Direction cosines of a line passing through 2 point

70

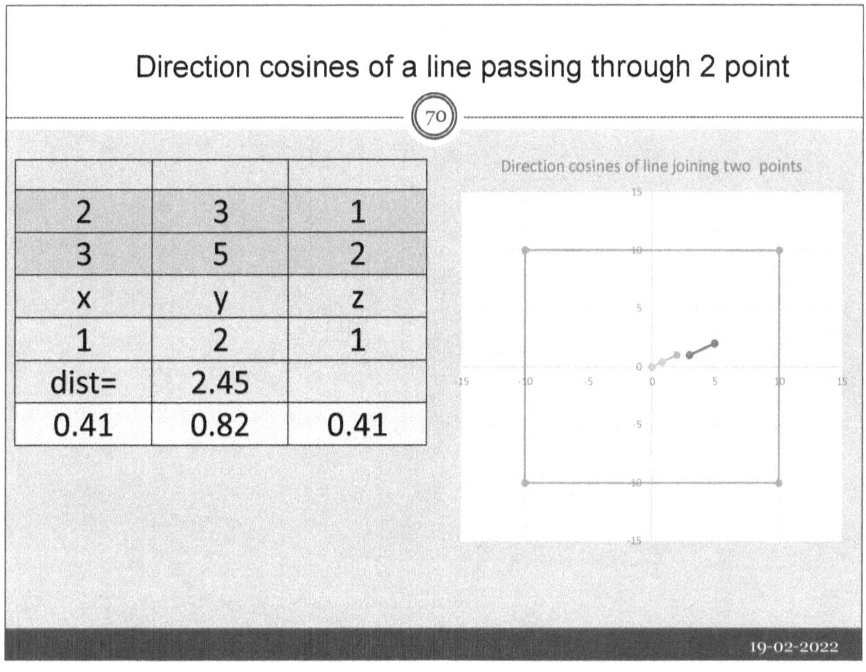

2	3	1
3	5	2
x	y	z
1	2	1
dist=	2.45	
0.41	0.82	0.41

19-02-2022

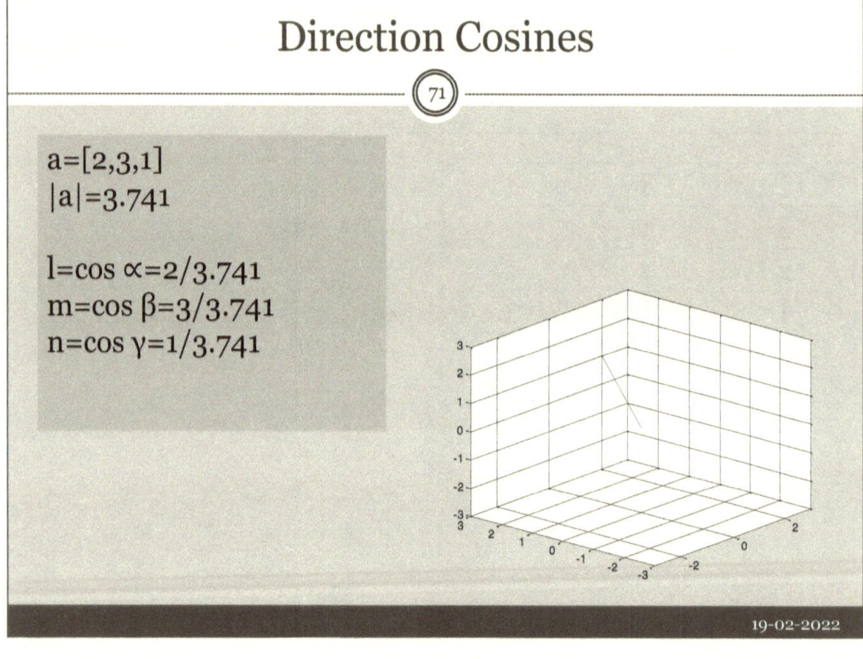
Direction Cosines
71
a=[2,3,1]
|a|=3.741

l=cos ∝=2/3.741
m=cos β=3/3.741
n=cos γ=1/3.741
3
2
1
0
-1
-2
-3
3
2
1
0
-1
-2
-3
2
0
-2
19-02-2022

Direction Ratios

a=[2,3,5]
r=|a|=6.1644
l=cos ∝=2/6.1644
m=cos β=3/6.1644
n=cos γ=5/6.1644
dir_cosins = 0.3244 0.4867 0.8111
angles = 1.2404 1.0625 0.6248
angles_degree = 71.0682 60.8784 35.7958

Direction Angles= ∝, β, γ
Direction Cosines=l, m, n = x/|a|, y/|a|, z/|a|
l=x/r, m=y/r, n=z/r
Direction Ratios=x, y, z=2, 3, 5
x=l r, y=m r, z= n r

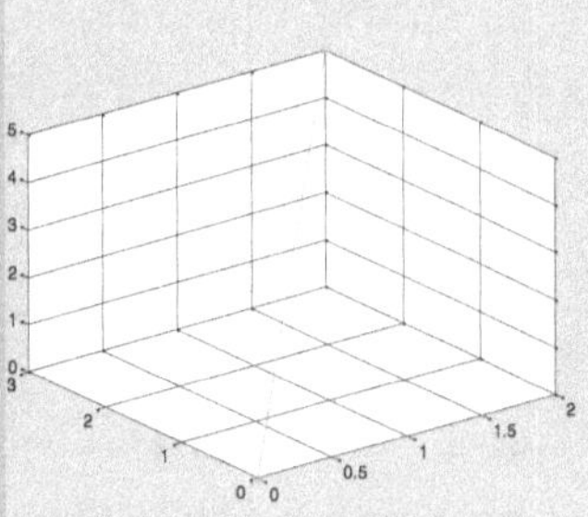

19-02-2022

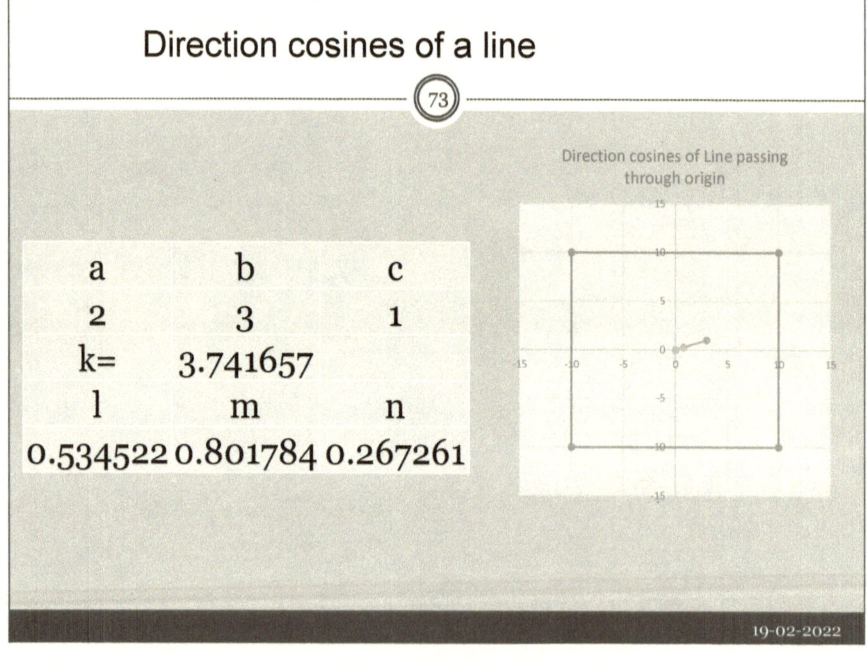
Direction cosines of a line

73

a   b   c
2   3   1
k=   3.741657
l   m   n
0.534522 0.801784   0.267261

Direction cosines of Line passing
through origin

19-02-2022

Equation of a line in space
(Vector representation of line)

(74)

- A line in 3d is uniquely determined if

1. it passes through given point and has given direction
2. It passes through given points

19-02-2022

Vector Equation of Line
Passing Through a point and parallel to a vector b

(75)

- A line passing through a given point and parallel to a given vector b:

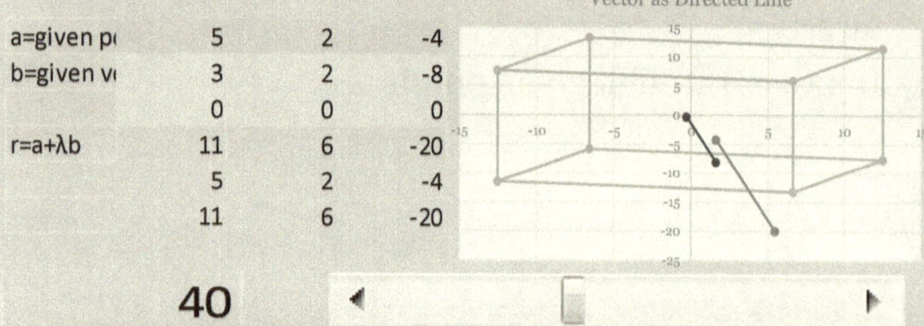

a=given p	5	2	-4
b=given v	3	2	-8
	0	0	0
r=a+λb	11	6	-20
	5	2	-4
	11	6	-20

40

We are required to find a vector r which will represent a line
From Triangular law of vector addition,
λb=r-a or r=a+λb, λ is a parameter and can assume any arbitrary value.

19-02-2022

Equation of Line
derivation of Cartesian form from vector form

Let the coordinate of given point A is (xo+yo+zo)
And Direction ratios of the line l are a, b, c

Then, a=xoi+yoj+zok
     b=ai+bj+zk
We have to find out, $r=xi+yj+zk=(xo+ \lambda a)i+(yo+ \lambda b)j+(zo+ \lambda c)k$

We know $r=a+\lambda b$, λ is a parameter and can assume any arbitrary value.

Hence, $x=xo+ \lambda a$
     $y=yo+ \lambda b$
     $z=zo+ \lambda c$
From this equations, we can write, $(x-xo)/a=(y-yo)/b= (z-zo)/c= \lambda$

19-02-2022

Example of the vector and Cartesian equation

- Find the vector and Cartesian equation of the line through the point a=(5, 2, -4) and which is parallel to the vector b=3i+2j-8k.

- Vector equation is r=a+λb
- Hence, r=5i+2j-4k+ λ * (3i+2j-8k)
- For Cartesian equation,
- r=xi+yj+zk=(5+3 λ)i+(2+2 λ)j+(-4-8)k
- (x-5)/3 = (y-2)/2=(z+4)/-8=t
- Parametric Equation: x=3t+5, y=2+2t. z=-4+8t

19-02-2022

Example of the vector and Cartesian equation

- Vector equation is r=a+λb
- Hence, r=5i+2j-4k+ λ * (3i+2j-8k)
- For Cartesian equation,
- r=xi+yj+zk=(5+3 λ)i+(2+2 λ)j+(-4-8)k
- (x-5)/3 = (y-2)/2=(z+4)/-8

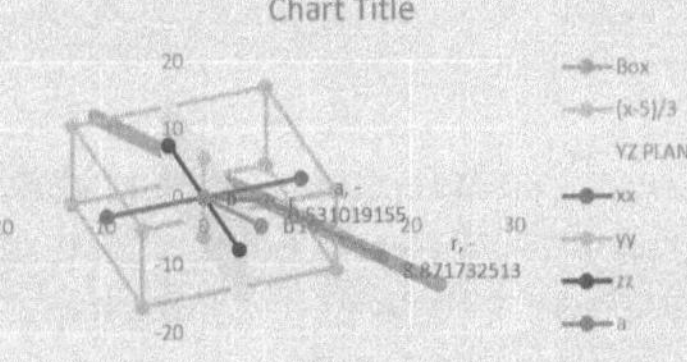

Vector Equation of Line
Passing Through Two points

(79)

- **A line passing through a given point and parallel to a given vector b:**

a=point1	-1	0	2
b=point2	3	4	6
	0	0	0

$r=a+\lambda(b-a)$

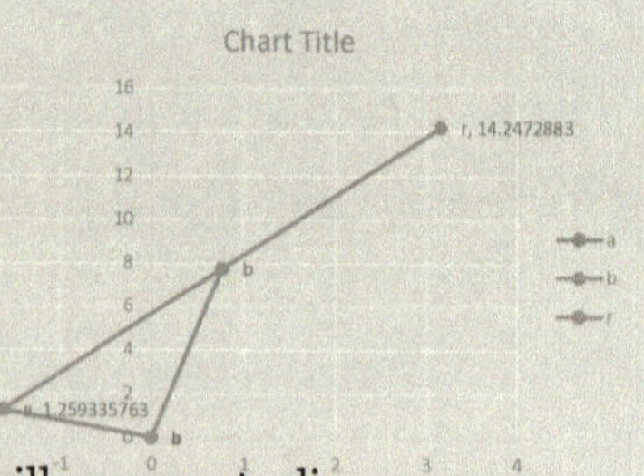

We are required to find a vector r which will represent a line
From Triangular law of vector addition and laws of scalar
multiplication, $\lambda(b-a) = (r-a)$ or $r=a+\lambda(b-a)$, λ is a parameter and can
assume any arbitrary value.

19-02-2022

Equation of Line
derivation of Cartesian form from vector form

Let the coordinate of given points are a=x1+y1+z1 and b=x2+y2+z2

Then, a=x1+y1+z1
$\qquad$ b=x2+y2+z2
We know r=a+λ(b-a), λ is a parameter and can assume any arbitrary value.

We have to find out, r=xi+yj+zk= a+λ(b-a)
=(x1+ λ (x2-x1))i+(y1+ λ(y2-y1)j+(z1+ λ(z2-z1))k

Hence, x=x1+ λ(x2-x1)
$\qquad$ y=y1+ λ(y2-y1)
$\qquad$ z=z1+ λ(z2-z1)
From this equations, we can write, (x-x1)/(x2-x1)=(y-y1)/(x2-x1)= (z-z1)/(x2-x1)

19-02-2022

Angle Between two Lines

Case-1: When lines pass from origin
Let l1=[a1, b1, c1] and l2=[a2, b2, c2] direction ratios

We know that the directed lines are vectors with components as a, b, c (a, b, c are direction ratios)

Now from dot product we can write, cos(t)=a.b/|a||b|
Or
cos(t)=|a1a2+b1b2+c1c2/((sqrt(a1^2+b1^2+c1^2)*sqrt(a2^2+b2^2+c2^2))|

19-02-2022

Angle Between two Lines

Case-2: When lines do not pass from origin

Let l1=[a1, b1, c1] and l2=[a2, b2, c2] direction ratios

Here we will take two line pass through origin and parallel to given line.

We know that the directed lines are vectors with components as a, b, c (a, b, c are direction ratios)

Now from dot product we can write, cos(t)=a.b/|a||b|

Or

cos(t)=|a1a2+b1b2+c1c2/((sqrt(a1^2+b1^2+c1^2)*sqrt(a2^2+b2^2+c2^2))|

19-02-2022

Angle Between two Lines

Case-3: When the direction cosines are given

Let $l1=[l1,m1, n1]$ and $l2=[l2, m2, n2]$ direction ratios
Here we will take two line pass through origin and parallel to given line.
We know that the directed lines are vectors with components as l,m,n

Now from dot product we can write, $\cos(t)=a.b/|a||b|$
Or
$\cos(t)=|l1l2+m1m2+n1n2/((sqrt(l1^2+m1^2+n1^2)*sqrt(l2^2+m2^2+n2^2))|$

19-02-2022

Chanchal Dass, FIE, Email: cdass01@gmail.com, Mobile: +91-8320172787

Angle Between two Lines

Case-4: When the angle is 90 degree
$|l_1l_2+m_1m_2+n_1n_2|=0$

Case-4: When the angle is 0 degree, the
$a_1/a_2=b_1/b_2=c_1/c_2$

19-02-2022

Shortest Distance Between Two Lines

- **Case-1:** When two lines intersect, then shortest distance is 0

- **Case-2:** When two lines are parallel- Then the distance between them is the perpendicular distance. This the length of the perpendicular drawn from a point in one line on the other line.

Shortest distance=0

Shortest distance= Perpendicular Distance

19-02-2022

Shortest Distance Between Two Lines

- Case-3: In space or 3d, there may be lines that are neither intersect nor parallel. These lines are non coplanar and called skew lines.

Shortest distance=
Perpendicular Distance

19-02-2022

Shortest Distance Between Two Skew Lines

- For skew lines, the line of shortest distance is the line perpendicular to both the lines

Shortest distance=
Perpendicular Distance

19-02-2022

Shortest Distance Between Two Skew Lines

- We know that the cross product gives us the perpendicular to both vectors
- Let, l1=a1+λb1 and l2=a2+μb2, Hence a1 and a2 are two points on lines l1 and l2. Let these points are S and T.
- Then the magnitude of the shortest distance vector will be equal to the projection of ST along the line of shortest distance.

19-02-2022

Shortest Distance Between Two Skew Lines

(89)

- For calculating the shortest, follow the following step

Given vectors are $l_1 = a_1 + \lambda b_1$ and $l_2 = a_2 + \mu b_2$

1. Step-1: Calculate the perpendicular Vector to b_1 and $b_2 = b_1 \times b_2$

2. Step-2: Calculate unit vector along $b_1 \times b_2 = b_1 \times b_2 / |b_1 \times b|$

3. Step-3: Calculate ST = $a_2 - a_1$

4. Step-4: Calculate d= ST cos(t)

19-02-2022

Shortest Distance Between Two Skew Lines

$$90$$

1. **Step-4: Calculate** $\cos(t) = \left|\dfrac{PQ.ST}{|PQ||ST|}\right|$

2. **Step-5: Calculate** $d = |ST|\cos(t) = |ST|\left|\dfrac{PQ.ST}{|PQ||ST|}\right|$

Or $d = \left|\dfrac{PQ.ST}{|PQ|}\right| = \left|\dfrac{b1xb2.(a2-a1)}{|b1xb2|}\right|$

19-02-2022

Shortest Distance Between Two Skew Lines

(91)

When the lines are in Cartesian form:

Then $l_1 = x-x_1/a_1 = y-y_1/b_1 = z-z_1/c_1$

And $l_2 = x-x_2/a_2 = y-y_2/a_2 = z-z_2/c_2$

Then, $d = \left| \dfrac{\begin{vmatrix} x_2-x_1 & y_2-y_1 & z_2-z_1 \\ a_1 & b_1 & c_1 \\ a_2 & b_2 & c_2 \end{vmatrix}}{sqrt(b_1c_2-b_2c_1)^2+(c_1a_2-c_2a_1)^2+(a_1b_2-b_1a_2)^{\wedge}2} \right|$

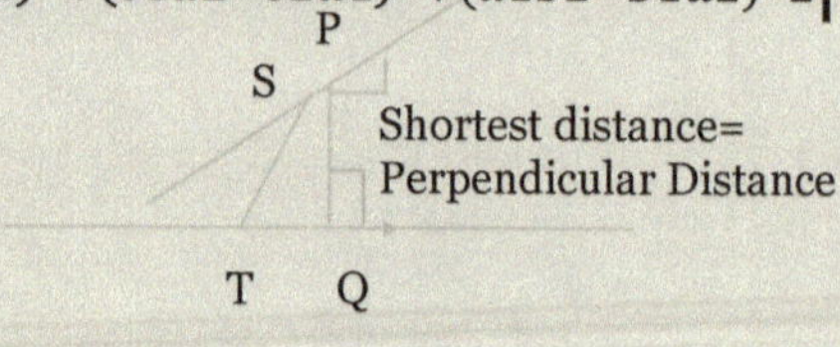

19-02-2022

Shortest Distance Between Parallel Lines

We know that the cross product gives us the perpendicular to both vectors
Let, l1=a1+λb and l2=a2+μb,

Hence a1 and a2 are two points on lines l1 and l2. Let these points are S and T.
As the lines are parallel then b is same for both the line

Then the magnitude of the shortest distance vector will be equal to the projection of ST along the line of shortest distance TP.

Let t be the angle between the vectors ST and b, then bxST=|b||ST|sin(t) n

Now ST=a2-a1
bx(a2-a1)=|b|PT*1
Hence, d=TP=|bx(a2-a1)/|b||

Shortest distance=
Perpendicular Distance

19-02-2022

Plane

- A plane is determined uniquely if any one of the following parameters is known:
  1. The normal of the plane and its distance from the origin. It is the equation of plane in normal form.
  2. It passes through a point and perpendicular of a given direction
  3. It passes through three given non collinear points

19-02-2022

Equation of a plane in normal form

- The normal of the plane and its distance from the origin is given. We have to find the equation of plane in normal form.

- Let the normal vector , v=a i+b j+ c k
- Perpendicular Distance of the plane from the origin is d

- First calculate unit normal vector, n= = v/|v|
- Consider a plane whose perpendicular distance (ON) from the origin is d and n is unit normal vector. Then ON = d n

- Let r be the position vector of the point P and P(x, y, z) be any point in the plane. Hence NP is perpendicular to ON.
- Hence dot product of ON and PN is o, i.e., ON.PN=o..........(i)
- Now, OP=ON+NP (Triangular Law of Vector Addition)
- Or r=d n+NP
- Or NP=r-d n....................(ii)
- Now, from (i), d n . (r-d n)=o, Or n.(r-d n)=o(As d≠o) Or n r- d n n =o
- Or n.r=d as (n.n=1)
- This is the vector form of the plane
  where n is the unit normal vector r is position vector OP
  or r = xi+yj+zk
The Cartesian form is
nx*x+ny*y+nz*z=d

19-02-2022

Drawing a plane in normal form

○ Given: The normal of the plane and its distance from the origin.

○ r . n=d

○ This is the vector form of the plane
○ To draw the plane, we require to convert it to Cartesian form:

nx*x+ny*y+nz*z=d

19-02-2022

Drawing a plane in normal form

```
Given normal is [2 -3 4] and the perpendicular distance =6/sqrt(29)

Unit normal- [2/sqrt(29) i-3/sqrt(29) j + 4/sqrt(29)
r.n=d
[x i + y j + z k].[0.371390676i-
0.557086015j+0.742781353k]=1.114172029
Or 0.371390676xi-0.557086015yj+ 0.742781353zk]
=1.114172029
For Plotting:xx=-5:.1:5
yy=xx'
[x,y]=meshgrid(xx,yy)
z=(1.114172029-0.371390676*x+0.557086015*y)/0.742781353
surf(x,y,z)
hold on
plot3([0 2],[0 -3],[0 4],'oy-')
plot3([0 0.371390676],[0 -0.557086015],[0
0.742781353],       )
```

19-02-2022

Drawing a plane in normal form

(97)

o The normal of the plane and its distance from the origin is given. It is required to find the equation of plane in normal form.

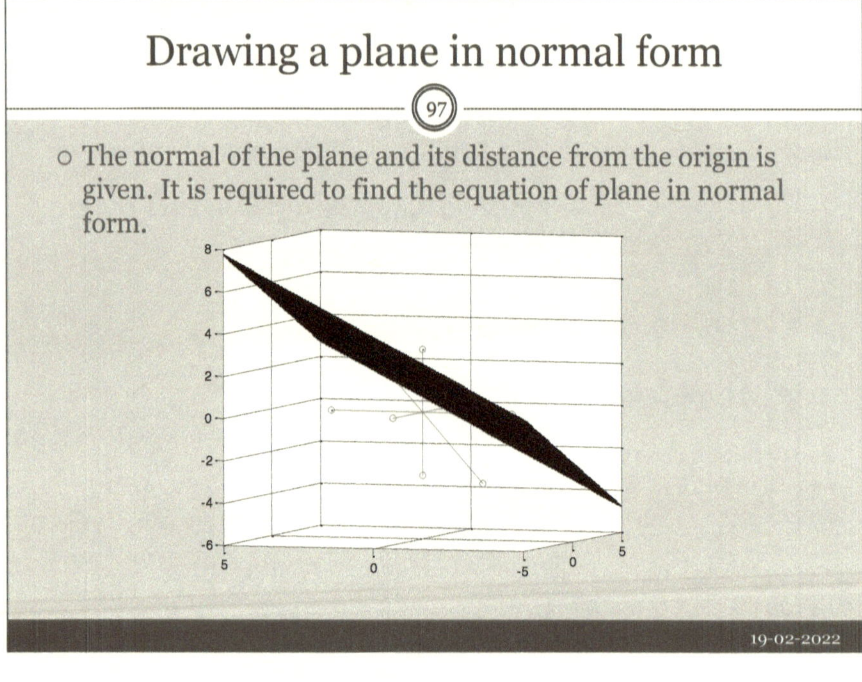

19-02-2022

Equation of a plane perpendicular to a given vector and passing through a given point

98

- There can be many planes that are perpendicular to the given vector. Through a given point $P(x_0, y_0, z_0)$, only one such plane exists.
- Let a plane pass through a point A with position vector a perpendicular to the vector N.
- Let r be the position vector of any point $P(x, y, z)$ in the plane.
- Then the point P lies in the plane if and only if AP is perpendicular to N, i.e., $AP.N = 0$.

19-02-2022

Equation of a plane perpendicular to a given vector and passing through a given point

（99）

- But AP=r-a.

- Therefore, (r-a).N=0
- Cartesian Form:
- Given Point A be (xo, yo, zo)
- Direction ratios of N=Ai+Bj+Ck
- r=xi+yj+zk
- (r-a).N=0
- So [(x-xo)i+(y-yo)j+(z-zo)k].[Ai+Bj+Ck]=0
- A(x-xo)+B(y-yo)+C(z-zo)=0

19-02-2022

Example

- Example-17 Find the vector and Cartesian equation of the plane passing through the point (5, 2, -4) and perpendicular to the line with direction ratios 2,3, -1.
- Point is (5,2,-4), hence Position vector is P=5i+2j-4k
- Normal vector N=2i+3j-k
- Let the Vector representing the plane R=xi+yj+zk
- From dot product, we get, (R-P).N=0
- Cartesian form:
- (x-5)*2+(y-2)*3+(z+4)*-1=0
- 2x+3y-z=20
- z=(20-2x-3y)/-1

19-02-2022

Example

- 2x+3y-z=20
- xx=-5:.1:5;
- yy=xx';
- [x,y]=meshgrid(xx,yy);
- z=(-20+2*x+3*y);
- surf(x,y,z)
- hold on
- plot3([0 2],[0 3],[0 -1],'^m-')

19-02-2022

There can be many plane to a perpendicular line

(102)

```
xx=-5:.1:5;
yy=xx';
[x,y]=meshgrid(xx,yy);
z=(-20+2*x+3*y);
surf(x,y,z)
hold on
plot3([0 2],[0 3],[0 -1],'^m-')
z1=(10-2*x-3*y)/-1;
z2=(30-2*x-3*y)/-1;
surf(x,y,z1)
surf(x,y,z2)
```

19-02-2022

Example

- Find the vector and Cartesian equations of the plane which passes through the point (5, 2, -4) and perpendicular to the line with direction ratios 2, 3, -1

Equation of a plane passing through three non collinear Points

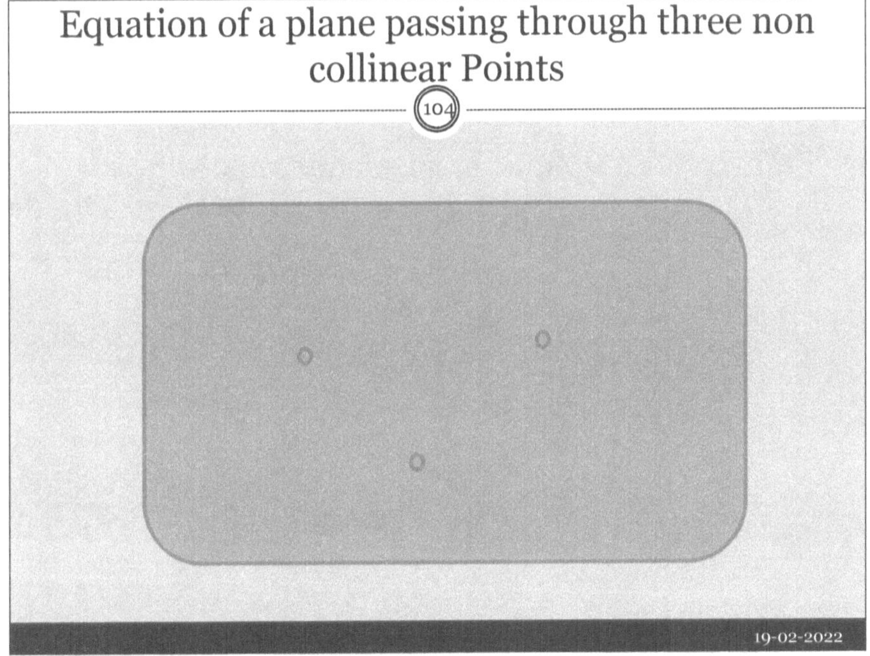

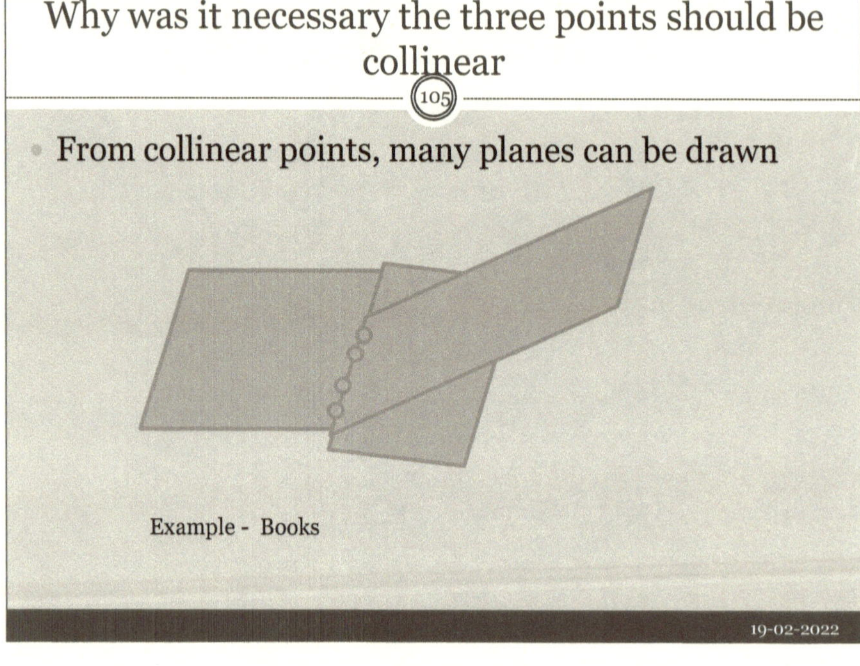

Why was it necessary the three points should be collinear
105
From collinear points, many planes can be drawn
Example - Books
19-02-2022

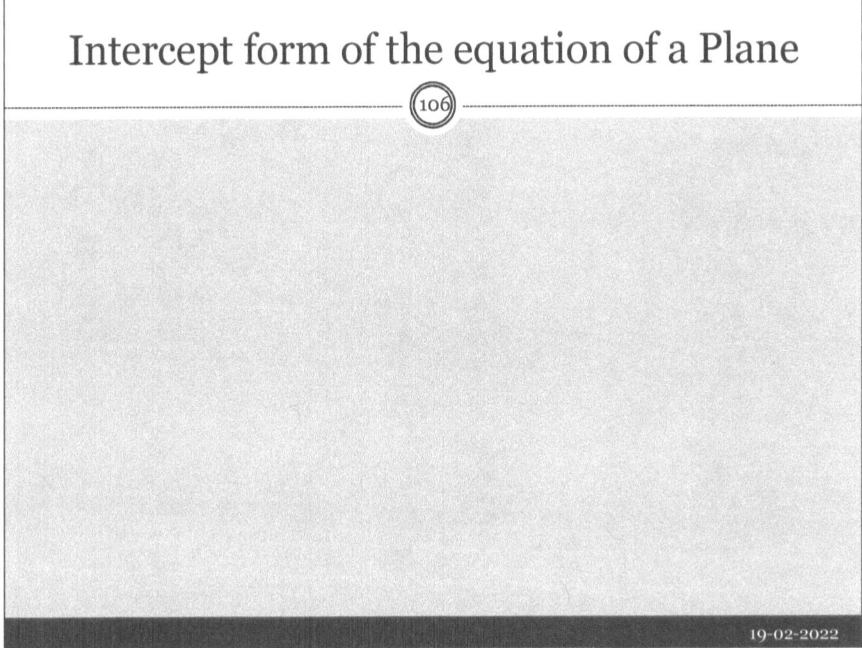
Intercept form of the equation of a Plane
106
19-02-2022

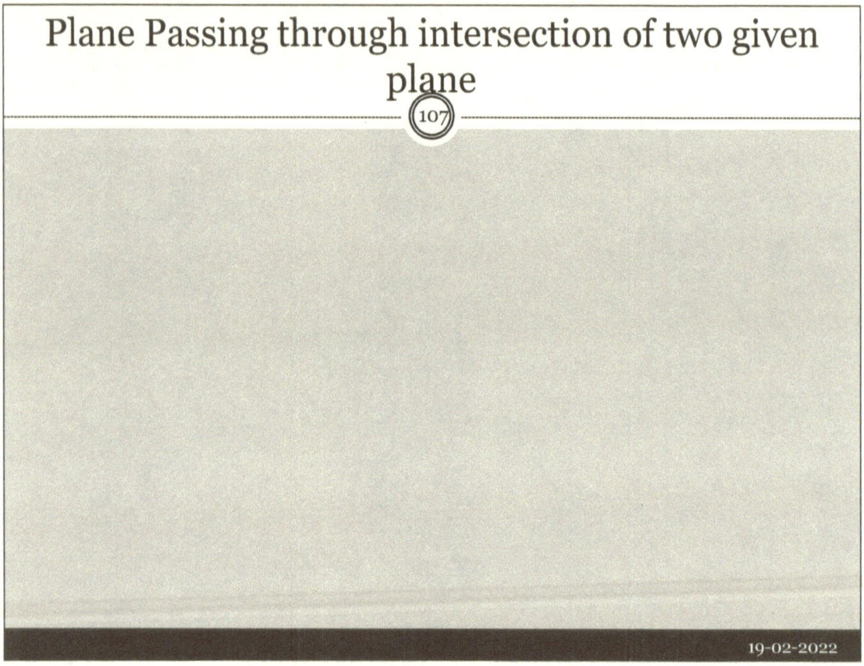

Plane Passing through intersection of two given plane

107

19-02-2022

Coplanarity of Two Lines
108
19-02-2022

Angle Between Two Planes

109

19-02-2022

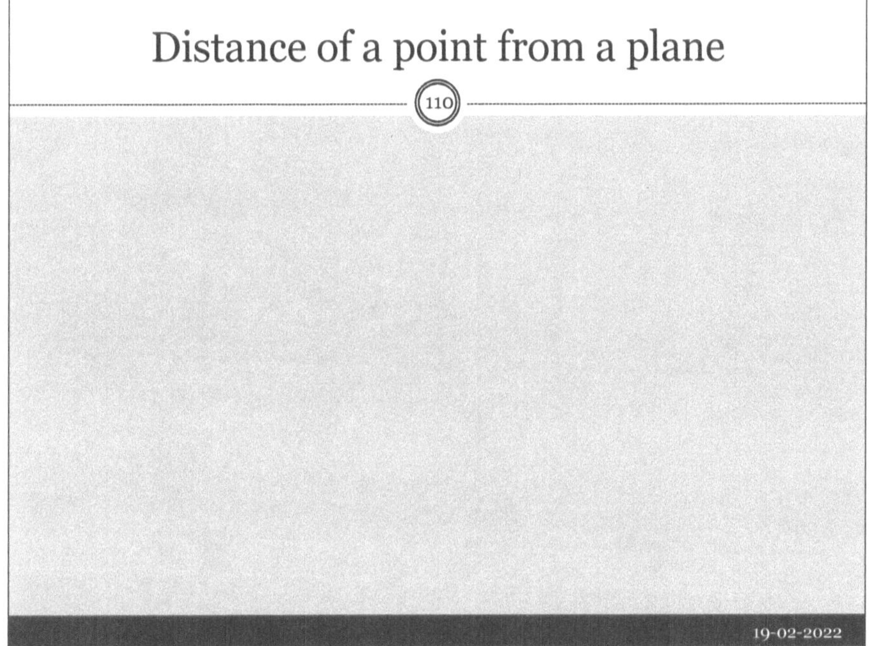

Distance of a point from a plane
110
19-02-2022

Angle between a line and a plane

19-02-2022

Bibliography

- Jones H., Computer Graphics through Key Mathematics. ISBN: 1-85233-422-3, Published by Springer
- Super Review of Calculus. ISBN-13: 978-0-7386-1106-8, Published by Research and Education Association (REA)
- Majewski M., Getting Started with MuPad. ISBN: 3-540-28635-7, Published by Springer
- Kreyszig E., Advanced Engineering Mathematics. ISBN: 81-224-0016-7, Published by Wiley
- Stewart J., Calculus with Early Transcendental Functions. ISBN: 81-3135-1980-5, Published by Cenage Learning
- Pratap R., Getting Started with MatLab. ISBN: 978-0-19-806919-5, Published by Oxford University Press
- Mortier S., 3DS MAX for Dummies. Published by Wiley
- Garrity T.A., All the Mathematics you missed. ISBN: 978-0-521-67034-0, Published by Cambridge University Press
- Vince J., Geometry for Computer Graphics. ISBN: 1-85233-834-2, Published by Springer
- Rogers D.F., Adams J.A., Mathematical Elements for Computer Graphics. ISBN-13: 978-0-07-048677-5, Published by Tata McGraw Hill
- Ygodsky M., Mathematical handbook higher mathematics. Published by Mir Publishers, Moscow
- Weir M.D, Hass J., Thomas' Calculus. ISBN: 978-93-325-4242-6, Published by Pearson
- Grewal B.S., Higher Engineering Mathematics. ISBN: 81-7409-084-3, Published by Khanna Publishers

Index

BEST PAPER AWARD

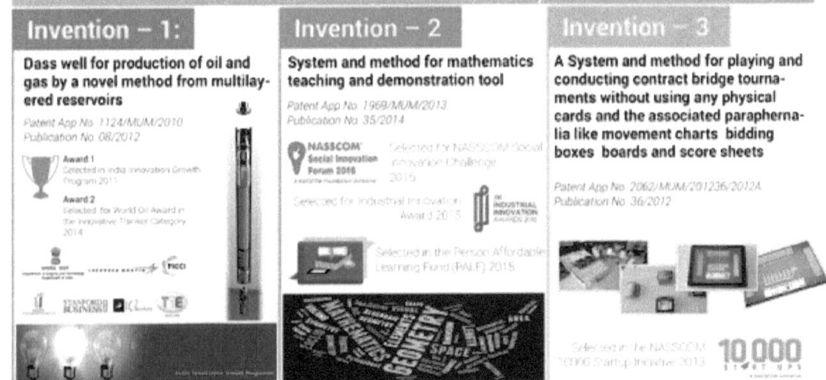

MY INNOVATIONS

AUTHOR WITH HONORABLE EDUCATION MINISTER OF INDIA

About Chanchal Dass, FIE, Author

I am a fellow of the Institution of Engineers (Mechanical Engineering) with Post Graduate Diploma in "Operations Research" and Master's Degree of Business Administration in Financial Management. I have started my career as a diploma engineer in Hindusthan Fertilizer Corporation Pvt. Ltd. and then worked in a position of Development Strategy Executive in ONGC, a national oil company of India, as a Reservoir Engineer. I am the inventor of Multiple Zone Well Completion Technology, Contract Bridge Gaming App and New system of Mathematics Teaching and Demonstration.

I am also a Life Member of Indian Mathematical Society, American Mathematical Society, London Mathematical Society, Ramanujan Mathematical Society, Calcutta Mathematical Society, Society of Petroleum Engineers (SPE) and Society of Petroleum Geophysicists (SPG).

I have published and presented numerous papers and attended various national and international conferences, forums and seminars. After separating from ONGC, I have established Dass Scientific Research Labs Pvt. Ltd. and Dass Oilfield Technologies Pvt. Ltd. for carrying out fundamental researches on different social problems.

I am a recipient of World Oil Award in Innovative Thinker category, SPE Regional Service Award, SPE President Award, ONGC Director/ Regional Director's Award, IIGP finalist, ICEBE Best Paper Award, Assocham Ericsson ICT Startup Award and many more.

I have visited many countries like USA (2), France (2), the Netherlands, Belgium, Germany, Egypt, China (3), Luxembourg, Switzerland, Qatar, Dubai (7), Abu Dhabi, Sharjah, Malaysia (4), Thailand (2), Singapore, Georgia, UK (2), Azerbaijan, Nepal, Bangladesh, Hong Kong, Sri Lanka, etc.

This is a technical paper. I feel that the readers may require the clarification of some points at some point in time. In that case, they may contact me directly.

My contact details are— Email: cdass01@gmail.com and Mobile: 9427030155

List of Institutions

List of institutions and universities where mathematics workshops/lectures were conducted:

1. National Institute of Oceanography, Goa, for research scholars.
2. Gujarat Technological University, Gujarat, for engineering college faculties as well as students (Around 20 Math Workshops).
3. Sahajanand Laser Technologies Limited, Gujarat, for practicing professionals.
4. Dhirubhai Ambani Institute of Information and Communication Technology, Gujarat, (3 Workshops) for Higher Secondary, B. Tech., M. Tech., and Ph. D. students.
5. Sri Padmavati Mahila Mahavidyalaya, Tirupati, for B. Sc. and M. Sc. (Maths) students.
6. Ganpat University, Gujarat, for B. Sc. (Maths) and M. Sc. (Maths) students.
7. eInfochips Training and Research Academy, Gujarat, for M. Tech. students.
8. Silver Oak College, Gujarat, for engineering students and faculties.
9. Venus International College, Gujarat, for B. Tech. students.
10. Gujarat University, Gujarat, for engineering college faculties from universities (RUSA sponsored workshop).
11. Indian Institute of Technology, Gandhinagar, for Ph. D. (Math) students.
12. Shri Swaminarayan Institute of Technology, Gandhinagar, for B. Tech. and M. Sc. students.
13. Kadi Sarva Vishwavidyalaya, Gandhinagar, B. Sc., M. Sc. students and university faculties.
14. Parul University, Vadodara, for university mathematics faculties.

15. Pandit Deendayal Petroleum University, Gandhinagar, for MBA students.
16. St. Xavier's College, Ahmedabad, for B. Sc. and M. Sc. (Maths) students.
17. University of Dhaka, for PG students and scientists.
18. Rayat Bahra University, Punjab, for faculties.
19. Chandigarh University, Punjab, for faculties.
20. Hotel Grande Delmon, Goa, for class ten to doctoral students and faculties.
21. I. K. Gujral Punjab Technical University, Punjab, for faculties.
22. Central University of Kashmir, Srinagar, for B. Sc. and M. Sc. math students.
23. University of Kashmir, Srinagar, for research scholars and mathematics faculties.
24. State Council for Educational Research and Training, Government of Goa, for school teachers.
25. Institution of Engineers, Maharashtra, State Centre, Mumbai, 2 workshops, open to all.
26. College of Engineering, Pune, Maharashtra, for university faculties and doctoral students.
27. Goa University, Panaji, Goa, open to all.
28. Institute of Chemical Technology, Mumbai, for students and faculties.
29. Indian Institute of Technology, Kanpur, for UG, PG and doctoral students.
30. Tribhuvan University, Nepal, for faculties and doctoral students.
31. Adani Institute of Infrastructure Technology, Ahmedabad, for UG students.
32. Indian Institute of Technology, Mumbai, for UG, PG and doctoral students.
33. Indian Institute of Technology, Kharagpur, IMS conference.
34. Indian Institute of Science and Educational Research, Pune, Time conference.

35. ICAPAM, Hotel Hilton, Dubai.